OUT OF STEP

WASHINGTON DC PUNK INTERVIEWS
BY DAVID A. ENSMINGER

SECOND EDITION

Much Misunderstood – Back and Forth with Brian Baker: From Left of the Dial No. 3, Summer 2003

When I ran into you at the Bad Religion show and you told me about the new Dag Nasty record, you described it as their Process of Belief in terms of how good everyone felt about the record, could you explain that a bit?

Well, I think that the *Process of Belief* is by far the best Bad Religion record I have ever been on and everybody knew in the band when we were making it that it was going to be very cool. We were really excited about it. Now, it comes out and it seems pretty much everyone else thinks it's the best record we've done since I have been in the band. With the Dag Nasty, I think it is pretty much the same thing. I really worked hard to try and make it a great record and everything fell together so great in the studio and while we were making it we were really excited and then once we finished it, everyone who has heard it has been like, Jesus, this the best thing you guys have done since *Can I Say*. I'm like, okay. That's why I made the comparison because it's a similar energy in the studio where everyone is just so fucking happy to be there. Talk about a smooth time when there's nothing to argue about because everything is so cool. That's when it is really fun.

What makes this record so different from 1992's *Four on the Floor*?

Four on the Floor was done like, well, basically, it's kind of explained in the liner notes. We didn't really plan on making a record, everyone was kind of hanging out in L.A., and we were like, maybe we should try and jam or something and the next thing you know Brett at Epitaph was like, you guys can make a record. So basically within ten days we tried to cobble together a bunch of songs, we didn't really get to rehearse, but ran into a studio and made a record that half of it is okay, but the other half really isn't. We really didn't put in the time and effort that is necessary to make a good record. It was kind of this fun vacation project and we weren't really thinking of it as something to carry on the legacy of Dag Nasty. It was more like someone recording us jamming and screwing around. There's a lot of songs on that record that are pieces of old songs that we had in 1985, and it just wasn't the same kind of thing. This record that we just did now, Minority Of One, we're definitely aware that we couldn't just put out another time, hi, we just felt like doing a record, thing. We needed it to be something we put a lot of effort into. I spent months writing this record, throwing away stuff and writing more stuff. We attacked this record like we had something to prove and I think we did, because I don't think that *Four on the Floor* is any good. I think it's a piece of shit, if you really want my opinion.

But even on the new record, you guys didn't play together until you hit the studio. At least that's how I understand it from the studio notes on the Dag Nasty web site?

It was the first time we were physically in a room together, but unlike the other experience, I had made copious demos, and everybody had all the songs for a long period of time. Everybody was doing independent study. It wasn't like everybody plugged in and was like, how does this song go? I mean, I made tapes of drum and bass without the guitar for Roger, I made guitar and bass tapes without drums for Colin, so those guys spent weeks and weeks learning the songs on their own, so when we came together we wouldn't have to waste expensive studio time. But, you know, the effort was still there. We just didn't happen to be rehearsing at the same time. This is not rocket science. These guys are good enough musicians, you don't really to…Well, you can do this on your own. It proved itself because we went and plugged in and said, okay, let's do this one song, and everybody played it. That was the whole point. There were some limitations with everyone living in different cities. It's kind of hard to get a good rehearsal schedule together.

Why did it feel like it was a good time and place to do it, instead of say, two years ago?

It's a combination of things. Basically, we did this compilation a few years ago.

1999?

Right, we got together to do that. It went really smooth and it was fun and that one song, to me, "Incinerate," was better than the entire *Four on the Floor* record and most of *Field Day* as far as I was concerned. That was just one song, and so when they came out as good as it did, and we had such a good time making it, we said, we said we should do another record at some point. And we were all like, yeah, let's do another record at some point and kind of left it at that. Well, Colin ran with that idea and he had a friend at Revelation who was basically hanging out with him and said, well, if you want to do a Dag Nasty record, I guess we'd do one. Colin called me up and said, you know if you want to do a record, we've got a label already without even having to look. I was like, that's cool, let's do another record, so we'll all agreed we'd do another one, but I kind of just kept procrastinating and screwing around. Eventually, last summer, right around the time I was about to leave to do the Bad Religion record, Colin said, look, are we doing this or not? Like put up or shut up. I said yes we are and from that point on I decided I was going to do everything I could and focus on doing it. So that's when I started writing. It was really Colin pushing me to do it, but not in a negative way, but it was kind of his whole thing. If Colin hadn't found the label and all this, we probably would not have done it. It wasn't like some master plan. Everything just fell into place and so we did it.

Dischord said it is completely coincidental that their re-issue (with extra tracks) of the first two Dag Nasty records and *Minority Of One* are coming out at the same time. How much input did you have on those re-releases?

Well, I was there for the re-mastering. I am the only one that still lives here really. Dave lives in Fredericksburg, but that's kind of like people living in Ojai and someone living in Silver Lake, it's so far away you don't see each other a whole lot. So I was kind of the one guy around, so I went with Ian when they were re-mastering it. As far as choosing the extra tracks on both of these things, basically that was kind of a group effort, but mostly Ian and I trying to collate the tracks and figuring out what extra songs we could find that were out there and put that stuff together. You know, the idea of having our friend Jason, who wound up doing the *Minority Of One* cover as well, has re-done the covers for the re-releases. So, I guess I was the one most involved with it, but it's a coincidence. It was really more a Dischord thing. Ian had the courtesy to let me get involved with it, but they were going to do it anyway. They are in the process of re-mastering virtually everything they have out that is still in print because when they re-mastered the first thing they did, which I think was the first Shudder to Think record, it sounded so amazing that they said they've got to do it for all of them. Dag Nasty was just on the list. There was no master plan at all.

Is there going to be a DVD combo of *Four on the Floor* and *Field Day*?

I don't know anything about that and I don't think that's true. *Field Day* is owned by somebody who isn't us, and I don't know anything about it.

What is it that sets Dag Nasty apart from other non-Minor Threat bands you were in, including Government Issue and Doggy Style?

Doggy Style was a joke, and Government Issue was a good D.C. band but didn't really tie together an era or anything. Dag Nasty, when you look back at it in retrospect, it was one of those first bands who could be a punk band that wasn't playing everything at a 100 miles per hour. Dave is such a really good singer that it was easy to write songs that weren't fast, because he didn't just yell, he could sing too. There were obviously bands like the Descendents who did that and were better than Dag Nasty ever was and are still better as far as I am concerned. They are one of my favorite bands on earth. There just were not a lot of bands like that around. Dag Nasty was pretty original when we came out. We had the pedigree of me being in Minor Threat and being on Dischord. Those two things certainly didn't hurt. That does a lot to sway public opinion, and Dischord has kept the records available in the record stores the entire time since 1985. You've always been able to get these records, and that helps too, because Government Issue stuff goes out of print, then somebody in Germany put it back out, then it goes away. Dag Nasty has been consistently available, and I figure that has a lot to do with why people are still interested in it.

Is there an element of truth to the conversations in fanzines during the mid-to-late 1980s about you having a master plan for Dag Nasty; for instance, you wanted the first record to be the best hardcore record around, then the following record to progress away from that until you made a great pop record?

There's an element of truth that I was aware that when I did *Can I Say* I had to make a really good punk record because, you know, I was keenly aware that being in Minor Threat meant that whatever I did next, people would pay more attention to it than if it was somebody who hadn't been in Minor Threat. I had an opportunity, and if wanted to continue playing in a band that got to tour, I didn't want to fuck that opportunity up. So, I definitely wanted to do...Well, *Can I Say* came out exactly as I planned it to, but as far as this long-range master plan, that's completely untrue. I didn't have anything past that, but I definitely sat down...When I started Dag Nasty, it started with me and a guitar, and I wrote down on a piece of paper that I wanted to do a fast band, I wanted a singer that doesn't yell, I got to find a singer that doesn't yell, and stuff like that. I was purposely trying to do what *Can I Say* became, but there was no long term, past *Can I Say* plan, and certainly when Dave left to go to Israel to go to school, any plans that we had were completely...That would have screwed everything up anyway because when we got Peter, who I think is awesome, but is a completely different kind of singer, we kind of just went on instinct and just did what we felt like. Some of it was good, and some it, sadly, was not.

Looking back, how do you feel now about the track on *Field Day* that pokes fun of the *Can I Say* era, like sampling Dave's line, "Twelve ounces of courage..." and laughing at it within the track. Was it really just good humor, or mocking the posi-core aspect of early Dag Nasty?

We were just having fun, and we were assholes. I was still a kid, and now when I look at it, it's kind of embarrassing and inappropriate because as an adult I certainly feel differently about the way people choose to live their lives. I think we were smart as kids and playing around for our own entertainment. We didn't really think of the terms that it was going to be on a record and available for the next 100 years. So, now I just think it's fucking stupid. I wouldn't do anything like that again because I think I am a little more of a grown up.

What do you think about the Shawn Brown demos that are still available from Selfless Records? Is that a viable period of Dag Nasty to you?

Yes, absolutely, and there's some Shawn stuff that I think is absolutely awesome. Shawn wasn't as good as a singer, but he was fucking awesome performer, and the yelling stuff he was great at. I think there's actually some of the faster songs I prefer Shawn's version too. I'm glad the stuff is out there, because it's all part of this whole thing. You take the good with the bad, and you can still buy *Field Day*, which I like half of it...Well, I can't believe that was where I was in my life and I thought that was a good idea. That's something I wish wasn't out there, but it is. The Shawn stuff is stuff I wish was pressed. I wish it were a record because I think it is great.

Now that Bad Religion has three guitarists, and let's say the new Dag Nasty record sells tens of thousands of copies, would there be an urge on your part to back away from Bad Religion and put more energy into Dag Nasty?

No. I am not going to tour with Dag Nasty. That's not what it is for. Dag Nasty is a writing outlet for me, because I don't write music for Bad Religion. And it's also something we do because we are friends and it's fun. I've never intended to jump on the reunion tour bandwagon. I don't want to sell a product. What I want to do is make records, and making this record was fun. I am really proud of it, but I don't want to go and try and market it. I am not a good marketer, and I have proven that many times in my life. But I think there's nothing I like more than recording. I haven't written any music in years, and I was just like, what the fuck has happened, I used to write songs. Everyday I would play guitar. I kind of got into this zone with Bad Religion because I wasn't really required to write, so I was just kind of lazy and playing guitar. That's what this Dag Nasty thing is an outlet for. I am not going to go on tour with it or turn it into some sort of empire. I am not interested in that.

How interested are you in keeping your other projects like the Doggy Style and Government Issue stuff in circulation. Would you re-visit those in terms of re-mastering and re-releasing them or playing a one off gig?

Well, I wouldn't do any gigs, and everything I've did, whether bad or good, I think should be out. I mean I would like to. I wouldn't put any personal energy into trying to convince somebody to re-release the Doggy Style record. If someone did, I wouldn't care. It's all posterity. For better or for worse, if I didn't do everything I did before I wouldn't be here right now. So I can just go back and say I don't want to hear that anymore. I would definitely be behind getting all that stuff out, but I certainly wouldn't be going on tour with it. It certainly is not my life's goal to make sure that that Government Issue EP *Make an Effort* is in every Tower Records.

Will this experience with Dag Nasty satiate your needs for a creative outlet for the time being, or urge you to do more things like this?

I don't know if my creative outlet will ever be satiated, I hope not. I would like to continue to do records under the name Dag Nasty because why the hell not, it's my name, I've got two tattoos, I mean, I might as well be in. I already have the fucking ink, I mean, some of them are even blurry! I want to continue to do this, and I've already started writing a couple of things and screwing around for the next Dag Nasty record. Basically, with Revelation, they are like, as long as you want to do this and we don't lose money, just keep doing whatever you want, which is exactly the relationship I want. I said, okay, as long as you don't lose money, I'll keep doing this. That's the plan I don't know, maybe we'll do one every two years for the next ten years. We'll be the Steely Dan of punk rock.

If this is the best period Bad Religion has found itself in a long time, where do you see it going from here?

Well, it's very much the same thing. The guitar player in my band owns the record label we're on, so I don't think we can get dropped. What we're going to do, is what we've been doing. I've been in the band eight years, and they've been doing it for 21 years, or however long it's been. We are going to keep making records and touring after the records are out until no one wants to see us play and nobody wants to hear the records or they are not any fun to make. It's the same thing. There is no marketing of Bad Religion. It's not necessary. Bad Religion is just what it is. There are people who come to shows that haven't bought a record since *Against the Grain*, but they go to the shows anyway. It's like this weird, for lack of a better term, and I hate this band, but it's this Grateful Dead thing, people dig Graffin, they dig what he's singing about, they like this music. It's astonishing to me how popular Bad Religion is and has been this entire time. I will continue to do it as long as there is a reason and people are into it. I mean, if Greg doesn't want to write anymore, I am not going to go, let's call it Good Religion and I'll throw some tunes down! It's really Greg and Brett's creative outlet, and it's nice to be in the position where it's also something the people want to see. I'm just going to do it as long as it seems viable. I don't really know. It's kind of tough. When you start a band in 1980, no one thought about what would happen 20 years later, because no one really thought there would be a band in 20 years. When you are fifteen in your mom's basement you never think that you would end up doing an interview in 2002. I don't know what the hell I am going to do.

But what does your mom think of you doing an interview in 2002?

Well, she's jazzed about it now because apparently I have been able to do it and not hit her up for money. Compared to most of her friends' kids, I'm doing pretty well. Initially, she wasn't too into it. She wanted me to go to this place called college, where you are supposed to go and then get jobs and stuff, but I didn't do that. I'm just lucky enough that I have been able not to hit up my parents for money. That's really the whole fucking goal, isn't it?

Is that one of the goals of punk rock? Not just to make music, but create a subculture where you can survive by making such music and doing things the way you want to do them?

I don't necessarily know it that's a tenet of punk rock, because most people can't. I mean, I don't think the goal should ever have been to be self-sustaining by the music, because that's not really very punk, because that means you are trying to create a product that you can live off of. What happened to me is a complete fucking accident.

You are the anomaly?

Totally, I am the *Minority Of One* basically, unless you count the guys in Fugazi. You know what I mean. I don't think that has anything to do with it. The whole concept of making money by playing music has ever been a motivational actor in any punk music that is any good. I sure know that whenever I tried to write a song to make money, it's been an embarrassing piece of shit. These are lessons you learn as you go through life. There is no way...Well, as soon as you try to point your art in a direction, your not an artist anymore, you're a marketer.

And there's a distinct difference between the two?

Because art is supposed to be, and using the term art, which I have only become comfortable using these last couple of years because I can't think of a better way of saying it, but what you're doing is expressing yourself and if there's a way other people can dig it, that's great, but you should be doing it whether other people are listening to it or not. If you are doing it in order for other people to buy it, that means you would have not done it otherwise.

So, you would get a job to pay your bills before you would make music to make money?

Of course, I've done that many times. It's not like I have been living off this for an entire 20 years. I've always had a job. It's just I'm lucky that recently I haven't had to have a job when I was off tour. But, of course, I would. I'm standing at my friend's motorcycle shop right now, and I'd probably just go put on an apron and start taking shit apart.

PIED PIPER PRESENTS
SCREAM
MURPHY'S LAW *FROM WASHINGTON, D.C.*
FROM QUEENS, N.Y.C.
ALL AGES
FROM CONNECTICUT...
76% UNCERTAIN
FROM WASHINGTON, D.C.
DAGNASTY
PLUS LONG ISLAND'S • CRIPPLED YOUTH
SUN FEB 23 4PM
LUPO'S HEARTBREAK HOTEL
PROV, RI

KELLY AND THE
ORPHEUM
FOUR BANDS
ALL PRESENTS SUMMER OPENER AGES
SHOW
FOUR BUCKS
DAG NASTY
§SPECIAL GUESTS§ STRESS RECORDING ARTISTS
U.S. DISTRESS
PLUS
A.F.O.
WITH
BEAUTIFUL BERT
AND THE CK'S
FOUR DOLLARS
KENOSHA, WISCONSIN
SUPPORT THE WISCONSIN UNDERGROUND SCENE... OK!!
BE THERE
EASY TO FIND
INFO: 1-414-652-6099
$4.00 WEDNESDAY JUNE 1ST
$4.00 DOORS OPEN 5:00 PM
4.00 5821-6TH AVENUE
4.00 IN/ON THE MALL DOWNTOWN
ONLY $4.00 CHEAP!
HEY! START YOUR SUMMER RIGHT!
UNDERGROUND THANK ALL OF YOU HAVE A GOOD TIME!!
ONLY $4.00!
CMON EVERYBODY!!
ALL AGES ALL AGES

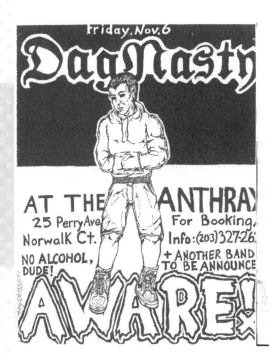

Friday, Nov. 6
DagNasty
AT THE ANTHRAX
25 Perry Ave
Norwalk Ct.
For Booking.
Info: (203) 327-262
NO ALCOHOL, DUDE!
+ ANOTHER BAND TO BE ANNOUNCE
A WARE!

COMBAT
C.O.C
CxOxC
CORROSION OF CONFORMITY
FROM WASHINGTON D.C.
DISCHORD
DAG NASTY
LUNG CHEEZE
11:55
WEDNESDAY JULY 25TH
THE GRAYSTONE
7816 MICH AVE. 581-1000
ALL AGES

$5 five dollars in ADVANCE

$6.00 AT the door

SUN. MAY 29th AT 126 15th Ave Polish Falcons Club:

TICKETS AVAILABLE AT:
Apple tree records
Rotation Station

No school the next day

w/ Inspector 12

DAGNASTY

UPCOMING SHOWS TO WATCH FOR
Ignited w/ Token Entry
Youth of Today
Underdog
Swiz + Lion D.C.
American Standard
S.N.F.U.

starts at 7:00
plus more B.Y.H.C. Zoo SKIP

EMBRACE
DAGNASTY
X SLAP SHOT X

BOSTON

AT THE RAT

SUN. APRIL 6 2:00

ALL AGES

TIED DOWN PRESENTS
X-MINOR THREAT
SEPT. 18th
DAGNASTY
CHRIST ON PARADE
soulside
OCT. 3rd D.C. core
PILSBURY H.C.
RKL
NEW JERSEY CRINGER
FLAG OF DEMCRACY
LOVE CANAL
EXCEL
infest
AT THE JACKIE ROBINSON YMCA
151. 45th Street SAN DIEGO!
INFO: (619) 705-6236
ADVANCE TICKETS AT OFF THE RECORD, LOU'S RECORD

THURSDAY FEBRUARY 6th
FROM D.C.
BEEFEATER
DAGNASTY
WITH BRIAN EX-MINOR THREAT!
HALF LIFE
ALL AGES
THE BANANA
3887, Brgslow Blvd

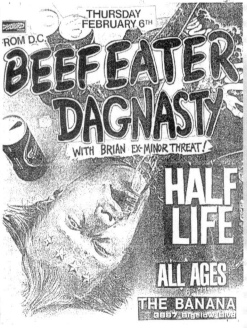

By Matt Dilg – Italy, 2004

From Bluetip to Retisonic – A Talk with Jason Farrell

Originally published in Left of the Dial No. 6, Summer 2003

Jason Farrell is a mythic figure that few people seem to pinpoint when discussing the legacy of Dischord Records, the label for whom he produced manifold album designs, including the post-modern packaging of bands like Fugazi. While Farrell undoubtedly contributed to the aesthetics of that generation, he also made sizzling records in bands like Swiz, whose brash late-hardcore prowess injected some bile back into Washington D.C.'s sometimes laconic late-1980's music breeds.

As a young gun, Farrell melded the sizable crunch of early Discharge with the frenetic unhinged dynamism of The Damned. Tunes like the under-produced "Time" and "Lie" blistered in frenzied, emotive, and inchoate onslaughts, helped by the cranky vocals of Shawn Brown, whose bark on tunes like "Taste"and "Stone" scrapes like sandpaper. Meanwhile, tunes like "Sunstroke" laid the groundwork for post-hardcore icons Quicksand and Snapcase.

As that band imploded, Farrell continued to design packaging and form bands like Fury and Sweetbelly Freakdown, which merited some attention. Once he emerged as singer/guitarist in the rock'n'roll inflected Bluetip, audiences

truly awakened to his uber-underground talents. Bluetip was like telling
Farrell, ready steady go. Four albums later, the work stands as testament to
his ability to dispatch songs with seemingly easy panache, merging hardcore's
neurons with smart rock'n'roll embellishments. The catalog is seminal, a nod
to procreative urges.

Yet, the prized possession of Farrell may actually be the mid-2000s gestated
Retisonic, a three-headed talent pool that combined Farrell's most nimble
pop-mindedness with the gymnastic drumming of Joe Gorelick, which is kept
in check by the throbbing bass plumbed by Jim Gimball. Their greatest slab,
Return to Me languished in a no man's land of small distributors, like the
French label Modern City. The 2004 material was a gem filtering Farrell's
past and present with uncanny skill sets. Tiny hints of Bay City Rollers, Gary
Numan, B-52s, and some Discharge and Minor Threat were tucked effortlessly
into the folds of the redoubtable album.

Robots Fucking, which was recorded during a 2005-2006 time table, revisited
this tempestuous territory with only slightly less robust production. "Wait …
Lookout!" takes aim at self-control, issuing fine observations with driving
beats and hallmark guitar riffage. "Airtight" pounces with a similar tempo,
though with some start and stop punctures and dizzying drums. By debating
themes like "blank life" and "living airtight," the song marks volatile
territory between fortitude and feebleness.

The pounding "Necropolitan" is a slab of poetic witnessing. The narrator,
or the public, for which the narrator is a surrogate, suffers an overdose of
"distractions/movie stars/sports teams" and "blind faith in technology,
religion, and nationality." The tune is damning and denunciating, relevant and
riling.

A few Swiz guitarisms surface on the power-pop with metal-edge "High on
Denial," which loosens up with a few handclaps, melodic urges, and ambient
spoken-word cuts that inhabit the distorted blitz. The ender, "Defined,"
comes on slow and sweet, with dimpled piano, layered and gauzy vocals, ample
assonance ("you can back track bones to birthdays"), and swaying swan song
rhythms.

**In the past, why did you seem to burn through drummers? What makes Joe
Gorelick different?**

I don't know. Bluetip wasn't a very well-oiled machine … nor was it a patient
entity. The majority thought "touring would solve everything," the minority
thought "I want to quit." Frustrations over these opposing theories resulted in
quitting before/during said tour. Many of the drummers Bluetip had were temps
for a specific tour, so you can't count them against us as signs of instability;
more like signs of our insistence to trudge on in the face of futility. We actually
wrote songs with three different drummers over our six years. I would say Dave
Bryson was Bluetip's definitive drummer (two albums and an EP, multiple tours
of U.S., Europe, and Japan). Joe Gorelick was Bluetip's drummer on our longest
tour (65 shows in 64 days) … He had joined just before we left and quit soon after.

**You've said, "Bluetip was supposed to be a multi-media collective… a
chance to bring the different artistic interest of its members (music,
graphics, film, carpentry, whatever…) together under one name. It
seemed like a good concept, but we quickly realized the music alone would
be quite a time and energy sponge, leaving little to wet other things."
Did you begin Retisonic with such ambitions, or does the very nature of**

the band (two members, total control) imply that you wanted something more narrow and stripped down not only in terms of music but overall vision?

Retisonic is a three-piece... Guitar, Bass, Drums. Jim Kimball joined shortly before our first tour. Joe and I wrote and recorded the "Lean Beat" EP before he joined. Retisonic has a simple theory: "waste no energy." We apply that to songwriting and song structure, touring schedules, practices... everything. A band can burn you out so fast if you let it. Running around in circles, letting off electricity like so much static causing little tiny shocks that seem random and unrelated. All that energy could have a much better effect if it could be focused into a single well-placed lightning bolt. Focus is key, and after many years of playing music, I'm finally seeing patterns, traps, ruts to be avoided. I'm also comfortable with the kind of music I write. It may not be groundbreaking putting a verse next to a chorus with some guitar over drums, but it does feel powerful, and I like it. As for the topic of total control: limiting input in songwriting and arrangement makes it all go so smoothly, and makes for a focused song.

"By the time I started writing lyrics for the *Polymer* **album I tried to broaden the scope of topics... getting away from autobiographical into fictional stuff. Like wizards and unicorns and how you can apply their nobleness to humans... set in futuristic outerspace. That way I don't feel so naked and exposed or whatever, airing my dirty laundry." In turn, however, the Retisonic lyrics seem more like realist-inspired, John Cassavetes-esque, concrete but poetic narratives, "Left the city proper, lost along the funeral parlors where the decade-old deli headlines read 'Shoot for Steady' ... " Was this a conscious move away from the style of your later Bluetip lyrics, or were many of the songs actually written during the same period, but fleshed out once you had the chance to concentrate on them without the internal friction of Bluetip?**

The second I get a lyric, I use it. Nothing sits around too long. I have quite a backlog of melodies needing words. So when ANY topic comes along that I might hammer onto a melody, I try. Unfortunately, I can't stand bad lyrics... I am extremely picky and it takes me forever to write something I think is OK. The Wizards and Unicorns thing didn't pan out so well, so it's back to reality.

Though none of the lyrics were from the Bluetip era, the first batch of Retisonic music was written before the last Bluetip tour. I wanted to slit the throat of Bluetip and fertilize the ground for Retisonic. I had Jake Kump (B'tip bassist) and Areif Sless-Kitain (the last B'tip drummer) join me in the studio for three new songs, two of which later landed on the Retisonic Radio EP. The opening song on the radio EP, "I Don't Drink (With Co-Workers)," is even older ... recorded with Dave Bryson, Dave Stern, and Jake. Bluetip had been given some free studio time, but had no new songs, so I asked the band to help me with one of my own, one that they didn't seem to like much. Otherwise, I would have gladly made it a Bluetip song (perfect example of the level of disagreement we had reached.)

Do you dislike touring the states (in comparison to Japan, etc.) because you are simply jaded to the U.S. circuit, or because you would rather immerse yourself in cultural differences and the challenges of being abroad?

In theory, I love touring the U.S. It's less expensive. It's right here. It's pretty. I'll tour most anywhere. Driving in Japan is a little bit less dull than driving in Iowa, but either way you're still just driving around. When you get there,

Jason Farrell by John Falls

you play the same songs. So the only real difference is the people who show up. There is something nice about experiencing a different culture, Japanese and European audiences in general can be more accepting and excited about bands... but that's way general. Harrisburg can be fun, and Chicago has made me smile. I don't consider myself jaded to the U.S. circuit... frustrated is a better term, but I'm not crying about it.

Do you feel that Bluetip and even Swiz, perhaps like older bands Rain, Reptile House, and Black Market Baby, are a bit under-represented in D.C. area history and somewhat shuffled to the side, even while being lauded by the U.K. press (Kerrang, for instance)? Why or why not?

Odd group of bands to throw Swiz and Bluetip in with. If Reptile House, Rain, or Black Market Baby seem under-represented, it's in direct correlation to their activity. I've seen all three bands. I think Rain played like 5 shows total. I remember Reptile House only because of Lungfish. BMB was pretty rad, but you're talking early 1980s. I don't know if any of those three bands even played outside the D.C./Baltimore area, whereas Bluetip and Swiz were first and foremost touring bands. I guess Swiz felt jilted by our hometown... but once we went on tour, we were treated like little ambassadors for D.C. As for Bluetip, whatever... we stayed together longer than 90% of the Dischord bands, put out four albums, toured all over the place... If we were shuffled to the side in someone's eyes, it's probably because they didn't like the music. And that's fine...

Your concern with technology and science seems to transcend mere song subjects. You've critiqued the, "...sense of accomplishment felt by everyone for how thoroughly we as a species have physically changed the earth. Our longest living legacy will be the chemicals and compounds we created that might ultimately kill us off. They'll last well beyond us, as a monument to our ingenuity and far-sightedness." Do you think that they will also be a monument to our short-sighted, over-zealous, and blind belief in science? Is that what you mean when you suggest that we, like Dr. Frankenstein, will be killed off by our creations/products?

Don't get me wrong: I'm not judging the human race for its short-sightedness, or for its blind belief in science. I don't really even fault people for throwing out tons of trash. When writing the song "Polymer" I was thinking of a parallel: yeast eating up all the sugar, shitting out alcohol, and dying in the environment it created. Yeast doesn't know any better. And in many ways I think people as a massive collection are dumb as yeast. The upshoot to the poisoning of the planet is the incredible accomplishment of permanently altering something. Making new compounds, like exotic liquers, to be drunk-up by a superior being. Human kind will live on through our creations/products... represented by the trace evidence, fossilized in polymers and plastics. That being semi-sarcastically said, I do find myself more concerned with recycling than ever. I can't just throw away paper.

Could you describe your ("North Rt.1" plus...) films? At one point you were "...desperately gathering up all the equipment we need, all the film stock, all the storylines we want to shoot and hopefully spend all ... summer...working on the record and working on the film. The whole plan was that it would all come from the same wellspring. You'd be able to cross-reference lyrics with storyline, film plot with soundtrack, let it all be this multi-layered thing."

Still a good idea. Just no time. I've made three films, and many shorts on super 8. Two were finished (The Tale of Kid Cadillac, and North Rt. 1) and the rest languish in my closet, taking up space with their reels and video tapes. It's hard enough finding time to work, practice, write, record, tour, and relax. If I could skip the "work" part, I'd probably be more productive... but maybe not. Everyone should have a dusty unfinished project in their closet... like a talisman that insures you complete the newer things you start.

I once saw a Make Up show at the Cooler in NYC (an event I believe was called "Destroy All Monsters"), which also featured a super 8 film, accompanied by a live music score by Brendan Canty. It felt as if the whole idea was to move away from a conventional rock approach, but now it appears that such a vibe has once again fallen to the wayside with the upsurge of new garage band success stories like The Hives and White Stripes. Do you prefer rock business as usual, or do you prefer to push the envelope with such multi-media shows?

I like rock shows. I always have. I like movies, too. But sticking them together doesn't always do it for me. I find flashing lights and projections to be distractions from the rock, which leads me to suspect that the rock is not up to par, and in desperate need of some camouflage. But that's just me. Some people don't like rock shows.

Many people, even unknowingly, have been an audience for your design, whether they buy Fugazi, Shudder to Think, and Make Up albums or albums by your own bands. Many of the bands are centered around Dischord. Would your design have a different trajectory and style if you would have grown up further outside D.C. and not witnessed the mid to late Dischord hardcore scene and the design of Jeff Nelson, whose work seems like a polar opposite of his contemporaries, like Pushead, Randy "Biscuit" Turner, Art Chantry, and John Yates?

Early on, Pushead was a far greater influence on me than Jeff Nelson. Pushead was all over Thrasher then: I'd draw the Zorlac graphics on my notebooks... I had no concept of doing graphic arts then. I just drew stuff. Once I got into layout and record design, I recognized how limited my output would be if I drew rotting skulls on punji sticks all the time... so I had to find more suitable role-models.

If the comic book found inside the first Swiz 7" is indicative of your early approach, at what point did you lean away from such a graphic style and move into the clean, almost minimal design of the Shudder To Think "Hit Liquor" 7 inch and your wealth of work, which seems close to the design aesthetic of labels like Teen Beat, Factory Records, and the modernism of the 1950s.

I wasn't even thinking back then. The first Swiz 7" cover was a direct lift of "Salad Days," minus any sophistication. The comic book that came inside was juvenile at best. I love it, I love thinking about what made me think it was a good idea. I didn't even like comics ... but that was the extent of my graphic knowledge at 17. By the time I was 22, I sort of knew what was going on and could recognize good vs. bad designs ... like most people, I found myself dabbling in the "modernist" thing, floating somewhere around 1960-63 school of thought ... Blue Note-meets-*Jetsons*. Still haven't fully kicked it ... but thankfully I never dipped into clip art.

Is it true that as you have pursued a music career more geared to your own total vision, your design for others has dropped a bit? "I do design covers for other bands, or help them in a less artistic fashion; just doing

the prep work for their ideas... all depends on how involved in their own aesthetics they are. I prefer HELPING as opposed to DOING..." Does this mean helping people like J. Robbins find their own design language and approach? The first thing I can remember him designing is the "Vehicle" 7 inch compilation.

"...dropped a bit?" I don't like the sound of that... this past year had me doing more record covers than ever. QUANTITY hasn't dropped, so you must mean QUALITY. Oh well. They can't all be gems.

I can design in any capacity: full-on control-freak to mindless automaton... whatever the project calls for. If I had to choose, I'd like a project to fall somewhere in the middle: Give me some direction, and act excited about my suggestion. Actually, the Burning Airlines *Identikit* thing I did with J. Robbins was pretty collaborative: he suggested the cross-like die-cut (originally full square panels), and explained what an *Identikit* was ... I took it from there, found a cover image, worked up a layout, cut the flaps back to get more "umph" from the die-cut, and made a bunch of fictitious "identikit" pages with adjectives pulled form his lyrics ("presidential" nose #4) ... It helps having someone as well-versed in design as J when working on a project.

Throughout the past decade you saw friends like Shudder to Think, Jawbox, and At-the-Drive-In sign to majors and quickly fade and fall apart. Yet, you've also befriended the Melvins ("angels") and Tool ("consistently amazing..."), who have survived bouts with major labels and earned much respect from fans and other musicians. Without falling prey to generalities or gossip, from your P.O.V. what made the former unable to bear the business? Was it entirely personality-led conflicts, or larger philosophical conflicts?

They were quirky bands. Quirky bands don't sell.

Jason Farrell Returns in Red Hare: Originally Published on Razorcake's website, May 2016

Featuring the core members of Swiz, the post-hardcore Washington D.C. band that bridged the 1980s-1990s with their tough-as-nails attitude, infectiously sing-along refrains, and nimble and voracious musical outpourings, Red Hare reveals the ageless angst that can still seize the night, especially when one enters middle-age doldrums. Irascible singer Shawn Brown, who first famously poured his viral vitriol onto crowds in blazing Dag Nasty, and combustible, insatiable guitarist Jason Farrell (Bluetip, Retisonic) join dizzying drummer Joe Gorelick (Garden Variety, Bluetip, Retisonic) and Swiz regular Dave Eight to shred all notions of retiring their chops and atavism. Dischord has not offered something as acerbic ("Fuck Your Career!"), acrid, and bitterly anthemic ("Be Half," "Dialed In"), minus their abundant and admirable re-issues of the likes of Government Issue and the Faith, in well over twenty years.

Yes, these same Swiz veterans tried something similar in Sweetbelly Freakdown, their mid-1990's project, but that effort felt a tad uninspired; whereas, this album blasts from the gates with teeth bared, replete with Farrell's sideways nod to mutant metal licks, Gorelick's effortless percussive punches, and Brown's steely street poetry on steroids. If this doesn't leave an ex-hardcore listener breathless, renewed, and invigorated, then he or she should return to a heap of retrograde vinyl platters and ignore the future. As the final, pummeling, bass heavy tune "Night of Midnite" (with Farrell dropping in for vocal) attests, it's time for people to take off their costumes, believe in whatever, run naked through their fears, and start living again. Swiz is dead: long live fiercely focused Red Hare.

By Brian Mishoe

By Brian Mishoe

Jason Farrell, Shawn Brown and Dave Eight

Tell me a little about the beginning of your music journey.

Jason: Growing up, I thought of music as this thing that you consumed. It was played by experts and marketed by geniuses in Hollywood and New York. I could get excited about AC/DC, KISS, Journey, et cetera. Wear their shirts, have an opinion as to how much Toto or Starship sucked ... but actually creating and releasing music was way beyond my comprehension. A short stint of acoustic guitar lessons playing "The Streets of Laredo" did little to demystify things. It wasn't until we all got into hardcore that things became more clear and possible. That scene lowered the bar and raised the encouragement level, giving people a chance to figure things out, even if they sucked in the process. Bethesda-Chevy Chase High School—and Bethesda, MD in general, had quite a few notable punks actively making music. Seeing them skulk through the school halls after having seen them play over the weekend further lowered the stage.

During this time, it seemed everyone was sharing what little information they had. My friend John Garrish learned how to play a bar chord, then turned around and showed me how to do it. That small gesture was the key to deconstructing most of the songs I grew up to, and helped me in creating my own. Lawrence McDonald was—and is—a great guitarist and skater who had played in Capital Punishment with Colin Sears (Dag Nasty) and Mike Fellows (Rites Of Spring) during the first wave of D.C. hardcore. He was instrumental in teaching music theory to me and many other skaters in our crew by bringing us into his band The Bells Of.

Plus you've stressed that women, often left out of narratives, were great scene ambassadors.

Jason: There were a ton of girls from the scene at our school: Maureen Gorman, Kate Samworth, Natalie Avery, Katie Chase, Jenny Mercurio. They were so sweet and supportive of our little group of skate rats just getting our punk feet wet. Being very active in the scene, they would point us to up-and-coming bands like Rites Of Spring, Dag Nasty; fill us in on the bands we missed like Faith, Minor Threat; and try to expand our taste a bit with bands outside the thin scope of D.C. hardcore like The Alarm, The Birthday Party, Bauhaus.

If you only go by the albums, then the D.C. scene seemed lopsidedly male. But those vinyl fossils don't tell the full story. Nor do histories about D.C. bands, if the focus is on bands and not audience. The heart of the D.C. scene—like many others—was social. The music was important for sure, but without the people, there wouldn't be a show. Most of my memories and I'd guess the memories of others going to these shows was of meeting people, seeing friends, hanging out on the stairs out front. It was a social hub of boys and girls talking, flirting, fighting, joking, smoking, trading anecdotes, et cetera... so females were there. And not just in a passive social capacity: they played in bands—Toni C., Sharon Cheslow, Fire Party, Nike Chix, Monica Madhouse, Jenny Toomey; booked shows—Cynthia Connelly, Pam, and Shawna; or were just infamous characters—Crass Mary, Lefty. Just look at *Banned in DC*, the first and perhaps best chronicle of the D.C. scene—compiled by three of its prominent women.

Jason, Dave, and Shawn, like others in the D.C. area scene—Henry Rollins, Ian MacKaye, Bert Queiroz, Kenny Inouye, Chris Stover, Eric Lagdameo, and more—you were skaters. As Jason has noted on doublecrossxx.com, "Skating and Hardcore were inextricably linked... it made the prospect of playing music seem more possible, logical, obvious..." How extensive was the crossover between the two D.C. area cultures/communities by the mid-'80s, and why do you think it's somewhat overlooked in D.C. histories?

Jason: To me and my friends, like all the people you name-checked, the skating came first. We then found the music that suited our activity. In the '80s, my Venn diagram of skating and hardcore was a solid black circle. And at the time, it seemed everyone had crossover to some degree. Not everyone was good or equally committed to either or both, but the two were common-law flirts. There was almost no need to mention one when speaking of the other, as they were two parts of one thing.

If the history of the crossover was overlooked, it was done so by those who left their skateboards in the closet along with their leather jackets. I'm not judging or begrudging punks who picked up a board for a few years only to drop it when Revolution Summer rolled along. As fun as skating is, not everyone can or should commit to it for life. And many skaters drifted in the opposite direction: going to shows to slam dance or get girls for a year or two only to fade on the whole thing. During my time in Swiz, my friend Chip, someone I had skated with and gone to shows with from the start, once said, "We all went through that hardcore phase, Jason... you just never grew out if it." He was saying it dismissively, but I took it a different way: skating and music are phases that many fall into and out of. I like to stay in phase with both as much as my life will allow.

On a blog, Jason describes the "blob" of his friends: skatecore youth exiting a station wagon, discovering the slam pit, smoking clove cigarettes, invading the nearby 7-Eleven during your first punk gig, Black Flag. In many ways, was forming a band an extension of that kind of wolf pack and brotherhood?

Dave Eight: Yes. Starting and learning to play music while becoming a punk was a completely natural progression. It kinda went hand in hand with skating. The magnetic attraction to both of these entities was unavoidable. We couldn't help ourselves.

Jason: Yes, the wolf pack vibe continued... but it wasn't the same group of people. By the time Swiz got going (1987), most of the core skaters I rode with since I was a kid had moved past punk. The formation of Swiz was random: Shawn and

I knew each other from shows and skating ditches, Alex and Nathan had been playing off and on for a bit, but when Ramsey Metcalf pulled us all together for our first practice, we had never all met. Despite not knowing each other, we didn't hesitate in giving a shot to a brotherhood of sorts. Ramsey didn't gel as well with the rest of us, so we asked him to leave. That moment solidified the unit, and we've remained tight friends—despite the breakup and distance—ever since.

I know you all started seeing punk gigs in D.C., but what about in Bethesda? Was Psychedelly still around, which—though not very open to hardcore punk—booked bands like The Razz and Slickee Boys?

Dave Eight: I saw Hüsker Dü touring for *Zen Arcade* at the Psychedelly in whatever year that was, 1984 or '85? I'd never been there before and was totally surprised to find it about a block away from our skate shop hangout The Sunshine House. The show was amazing, maybe twenty people there. I remember Bob Mould asking somebody from the twenty of us to come up and help sing the song, "Somewhere" cause he couldn't do it and play guitar very well at the same time. Grant Hart was wearing a purple silk shirt. Greg Norton had that wacky mustache and played the bass with three fingers. They were different and rad and super-intense without being pretentious. Great show.

Jason: The second show I ever saw was TSOL and No Trend at the Psychedelly on a Saturday afternoon in the spring of '84. Chip and I were the only members of B.S.R. (Bethesda Skate Rats) around that day. We were still quite new to the punk thing and didn't really have the wardrobe. In preparation, Chip had cut the sleeves off the pink long sleeve shirt he was wearing, but kept the sleeve ends as bracelets. He drew cufflinks on them with a sharpie—affecting a Snagglepuss look. I may have messed up my hair. We were the only pre-pubes at a show that consisted of at most ten people: the bands, Chip, me, and Ian Mackaye. The singer of No Trend spent a very long time hanging a sheet from the ceiling to obstruct the audience's view, then spent the set with his back turned. I don't remember TSOL's set. It was just an awkward daytime show in sleepy downtown Bethesda at a tiny bar/sandwich shop—a stark contrast to the sweaty, packed, dangerous, and exciting Black Flag show we had just seen somewhere deep in D.C.

A year or so later there were shows being held at the Bethesda Community Center and the nearby Chevy Chase Community Center. I remember seeing some great shows with Rites Of Spring, Lunchmeat, Embrace, Bells Of, Mission Impossible, and others spread out over the summer—the "revolution" one. I recall a few more happening in the years that followed—Rain, Swiz, At Wits End, maybe even Ignition?

***Dance of Days* paints a picture of leftist Bethesda youth, many later Dischord-affiliated, listening to Crass, Poison Girls, and Zounds, who founded short-lived bands like Fungus Of Terror, Bozo Brigade, and Gang Of Intellectuals. Were you aware of these locals, bands, and their tastes?**

Dave Eight: Nope.
Jason: Not really. I recall hearing those names. Of the small Bethesda bands, I remember Bloody Mannequin Orchestra—Colin and Roger who later played in Dag Nasty—but mostly because Colin lived in my neighborhood a couple streets away. And Bells Of...

Jason and Shawn, if being in Bells Of... and Dag Nasty shaped your musical growth—from nothing to something!—did it also pave your way into D.C., or did you still feel an outsider's perspective that perhaps later shaped your music and art?

Shawn: I guess being in Dag Nasty and later in Swiz did pave our way into the D.C. scene, and that scene definitely influenced us. How could it not? All we did was hang out downtown back then. That being said, coming from outside of the city (nearby Hyattsville, MD) we had a little bit different perspective, so maybe we were more like outsider-insiders.

Jason: Playing second guitar and then bass in Bells Of (...) was my first band experience. I was fifteen and would sit in on Bells Of practices occasionally, waiting for Lawrence (guitarist and band leader) to finish so I could get a ride to the ramp. Alec MacKaye (Faith) was still their singer then—he soon quit, just before their second show (opening for Rites Of Spring and Embrace). Lawrence decided to take over singing along with guitar, and told me I was now in the band as second guitar. This was something I wasn't expecting and probably wasn't ready for, but I was happy to get the chance to play with two of my favorite bands.

Learning about music through Lawrence definitely started me on my own way into music, but it wasn't a yellow brick road into the inner scene of D.C. Somehow Bells Of never got much acceptance in the scene, nor did my following band Swiz. That's not to say that Swiz didn't have any people at our shows, or any help. Amanda MacKaye was out biggest supporter—personally and through her label Sammich—and Dischord helped her fund Swiz releases, but we did feel palpable disinterest from the D.C. scene. I don't know why this came as a surprise to us—our music was more in line with a sound the current scene was doing everything to abandon—but we took the rejection personally. It fueled us to dive deeper into the aggressive sound we started out with, rather than swing to the more experimental sounds like Soul Side and Shudder To Think or softer sounds of the era. After Swiz broke up, I was more actively designing record covers (Severin, Circus Lupus, Fugazi, Lungfish, Trusty, Fireparty) and that gave me the opportunity to shape my art/aesthetic, which has led to a career. I owe a big debt to Dischord for that and feel honored each time they ask me to work on a new cover.

Though Swiz missed being part of Revolution Summer, do you feel the band carried forward that ethos?

Dave Eight: I hope this doesn't start a fight, but I still feel like Revolution Summer is bigger in legend than it was as a movement at the time. We went to see Rites Of Spring down at Food For Thought. Great show. I think somebody told me about Revolution Summer there, although I'm not sure I really understood what they were talking about. Car-less and broke, I think we walked two hours back to Bethesda from Food For Thought that night.

To me, I don't really think the ethos of Revolution Summer ever felt different than what was already instilled in 1983 from my first listen to Out of Step (Minor Threat), Still Screaming (Scream), Subject to Change (Faith), Joy Ride (Government Issue), No Policy (SOA) and Minor Disturbance (Teen Idles) EPs, My War (Black Flag), Lullabies Help the Brain Grow (Big Boys), Golden Shower of Hits (Circle Jerks), Paranoid Time (Minutemen), and Metal Circus (Hüsker Dü). Yeah, maybe I'm a bit off topic here. It wasn't conscious, but I do feel like we carried an ethos of what was learned on that first group of punk records we all gathered.

Shawn: Swiz wasn't an extension of that thought process. I mean, we had songs that were a bit more personal and inner-driven like bands of that time, but there was also a lot of political stuff they were doing, topics we might have touched on, but it wasn't really our main drive. Swiz was maybe quasi-political at most.

Jason Farrell by Matt Dilg - England, 2004

Jason: As much as I loved the bands, music, and shows I saw from that era, Swiz wasn't carrying on the Revolution Summer baton a year or two later. Influences were definitely there. Mike Hampton of Embrace is a phenomenal guitar player who certainly influenced me quite a bit. If anything, we were hoping to carry on the broader ethos of D.C. music, tapping in back to the Faith, Void, Minor Threat. Our position, compared to Rites Of Spring and Embrace, was more like an alternate parallel than episodic and linear—fancy talk—but I wouldn't be putting Swiz up with any of those bands in terms of impact or importance. Hopefully we weren't too much like a Neanderthal cousin that managed to survive.

D.C. punk always seemed so diverse and inclusive to many of us growing up in Middle America, yet Fred "Freak" Smith (Beefeater) mentioned D.C. should have been even more diverse, given its demographics. As a touring band that scoured the country, did you feel D.C. was special, different? Like an anomaly?

Shawn: Yes. I'll just say that. Yes.

Dave Eight: Okay, first of all, when did the "freak" name sneak in there? Jason and I have said before how glad we were to grow up in D.C. and we felt honored to be close to the music scene there. I think for a long time I really didn't think about bands outside of D.C., except for a couple in California and the Big Boys in Texas, or the Damned and Discharge. And then I discovered the Minutemen and a couple other things and slowly became aware that there were many other scenes around the country. It kinda made me realize I was a bit narrow minded toward D.C. stuff. It's tough 'cause there was so much great music in D.C. I kinda didn't think to look elsewhere. I mean, after you witness Void at the Wilson Center, you don't really need to search out much else. It takes some time to come down off that sound.

Jason: The D.C. suburban area was very diverse. The diplomats and international status of the city brought exposure to many different cultures. D.C. as a city was predominantly black—seventy-eighty percent?—with the minority of whites huddled in the Northwest quadrant. This is where the hardcore scene emanated. Perhaps as a result, the D.C. scene was very white, like most punk scenes. I agree with Fred that it could have or should have been more diverse, but I do feel the scene was accepting of anyone who showed up: black or Asian or Hispanic punks were just punks first and foremost.

When opening for Public Enemy, did you feel that such a crossover audience was sustainable, perhaps somewhat like Scream and Minor Threat doing the Trouble Funk gigs?

Dave Eight: I wish I'd gotten to play this show. Damn you Nathan (Larson, who replaced Dave on bass)!

Jason: I was just happy to be opening for Public Enemy.

Shawn: I definitely remember a lot of punks being there, and hip-hop people who were straight up into PE, plus a bunch of suburban kids. Yeah, it was a crossover. I don't know if anyone else thought of it, but it definitely made me think of the Minor Threat / Trouble Funk show.

Jason: I don't know if it meant anything to the hip-hop crowd, but for the punks into PE and Swiz they were just like, "I can't believe this is happening."
Shawn: Oh yeah, that shit was legendary. Definitely one of the highlights of our career.

Unlike many D.C. bands, Swiz was touring constantly. Was this something inspired by locals like Government Issue and Scream, your own burning desire to hit the road, or maybe your quest for new places to skate as well?

Dave Eight: During our first show we saw, Black Flag touring for *My War*, I remember Rollins saying—possibly bragging—that they we're gonna tour Europe soon after the show we were at. That was maybe the coolest thing I'd ever heard. At that moment, I knew, without a doubt, that's what I wanted to do. My goal/dream/purpose in life would be to play loud fast music, put out records, and tour. Simple.

Jason: We played out of town because we wanted to play a lot. You could only play maybe once a month in D.C., and for a while it didn't seem like D.C. even wanted that much out of us. So, we'd take weekend trips out to Boston, N.Y.C., Norwalk, Rochester, Harrisburg, Richmond, Norfolk, Providence, anywhere that would have us. The shows were better received, so we kept coming back.

We did two full U.S. tours: on the first one in 1988 we tagged along with Soul Side and American Standard on their already-existing tour to California. We didn't have anything planned for the way back, and our van broke down on our way to the last show anyway—we were too young to know about standard maintenance things like transmission fluid—trapping us in San Francisco for two weeks. By the second tour in summer of 1989 with Shudder To Think, we had gotten the whole maintenance thing under control, but the whole tour was poorly planned and left us demoralized.

Apart from the blistering speed of the first single, the two albums really explore slower, methodical tempos, like in the song "Cakewalk." Swiz slowed down during the same time as Verbal Assault. Did you make a conscious decision to shed old song habits and seek something new? Was it a reaction to Fugazi, Fire Party, and late-period Scream?

Jason: I always argued for aggressive songs with faster tempos. It's a fun way to play. Thankfully, my limited vision was tempered by Nathan and Alex's willingness to be more experimental. The song "Sunstroke" was the first time I lost my speed battle against those two. I'm glad they won. From that point on, we wrote whatever came out and at whatever speed it issued forth. "Cakewalk" was one of the last songs we wrote. Bad Brains' *Quickness* had just come out. The opening track "Soul Craft" is so powerful and methodical, I had to rip it off.

Shawn: I think we were just writing songs, you know? We wanted to have a couple of songs that would give us a break in playing, give all the songs and us a chance to breathe. It wasn't a reaction to Fugazi or Verbal Assault at all.

How would you describe the difference between Sammich, run by Amanda MacKaye, and Dischord, run by her brother Ian and Jeff Nelson?

Shawn: Well, Sammich was just beginning and Dischord had been around for a bit. (laughs)

Jason: Dischord was "big" and is still around, Sammich was "small" and is now gone. Sammich was lazily viewed as the little sister label to Dischord—shorthand answer mirroring the real-life relationship of Ian and Amanda—but I don't think that's a fair assessment. Amanda, along with Eli Janney in Sammich's early form, should be given more credit for having debuted some of D.C.'s most noteworthy artists like Soul Side, Shudder To Think, and Dave Grohl's humble beginnings in Mission Impossible.

Dave Eight: Dischord and Sammich are two different things but not far apart at all. It felt like Amanda was actually in Swiz, which was great. She came to the shows with us, helped us get paid. She was kind of a mentor/manager. Let alone she could give and take just as much shit as the rest of us, which of course is a natural part of touring. Being on Dischord with Bluetip was a dream come true. With Bluetip, it felt like we were a touch more separate from the label, but that was actually good because we were actually ready, for better for worse, to be more on our own and to figure out more how we liked to do things. In retrospect, maybe Bluetip shoulda taken Amanda on the road also. We could have used a solid ref (laughter).

Both Jason and Shawn have talked about the ugly side of D.C. punk—the skinhead scene that simmered—and *Dance of Days* suggests Swiz tunes like "Tylenol" were a form of defiance. Why did such a scene happen amid a city full of Punk Percussion Protests and Positive Force benefits?

Jason: Because everywhere has assholes.

Shawn: "Tylenol" wasn't about that. Why did that skinhead scene happen within the D.C. scene? Because people have different interests, and because people are attracted to different stuff. Skinhead was always a thing in D.C. It wasn't necessarily always a negative thing. Yes, we had some negative people that were in the skinhead scene, but I knew skinheads who were just into being working-class people, y'know? I think every punk scene had that. I mean, you have to remember we're talking about punk rock: no rules, no one is telling you what to do, so people are going to do all kinds of stuff. Yes, there was a knucklehead side to it that really came out in the late '80s, I understand that, but as far as being begrudging to skinheads in general, I'm not, because a lot of my friends were skinheads. I wish somebody would explore that whole thing more, because there's a lot of shit I don't know about, a lot of shit I'm interested in. Like, what were those guys trying to do? Or were they trying to do anything? What was their philosophy? What's the attraction, and what did they get out of it?

In some ways, does the Red Hare song "Message to the Brick" also involve complicated (or not-so-complicated) issues of race in lines like, "money preying on a misplaced sense of pride and need for identity"? Though ethnicity is not specifically mentioned, the innuendo seems to suggest power-hungry politicians seek black votes; or is it simply about all voters being merely a numbers game?

Jason: You could read it that way—white Democratic politicians paying lip service to black and Latino voters—but I was talking about the Republican side. White politicians seeking white votes, stirring up racism, patriotism, or whatever sticks to get poor people to support platforms that are directly counter to their own self interest. It's a fantasy piece where the scam is revealed and the dupe wakes up. Based on current polls, it would seem a bunch of people are still asleep.

Red Hare and Swiz engage anger; in Swiz, the anger is palpable, boiling both on the surface and pushing the themes, emotions, and musical force. Red Hare songs like "Horace" ("holding on to pent up shit from twenty years ago") and "Be Half" ("stop being angry / it's what you want"), the band seems to interrogate anger. Is that a kind of wisdom that comes from aging, or a way to recognize that anger is not always the right energy?

Shawn: I think it's both. It's wisdom, and trying to understand where that shit comes from.

Jason: Calling out bullshit and hypocrisy in yourself and in others is a classic lyrical theme in punk and hardcore. Anger—or sarcasm—is the reaction to that topic, it's not the topic itself. Both Swiz and Red Hare approach the topic the same way: from a personal perspective. The perspectives of a nineteen year old and a forty five year old are very different. As a result, the songs of Swiz and Red Hare are different despite sometimes sharing similar topics.

Jason had a "twin love of Metallica and Faith" plus liked the crunch of Discharge, and Swiz reflects that—searing guitar, propulsive drums, and antagonistic but intelligent vocals. Yet, a secret ingredient in Swiz and Red Hare is sublimated new wave: Shawn's early taste for B-52's, Jason for Gary Numan. To me, this seems to create a slanted, rhythmically twisted version of guitar rock.

Dave Eight: Don't forget the goth! I believe the era of music from the late 1970s to the mid-'80s—there was so much great stuff. The Damned crossed so many genres: punk, new wave, and goth. I kinda think they made it easy to open our ears to bands like Devo and Bauhaus.

Jason: You are spot on. Yeah, I love the guitar chubb-chubb stuff. It's really fun to play and can be exhilarating to hear. But I like a lot of stuff—new wave, goth, rock—and have shamelessly lifted from Love And Rockets, The Cult, Gary Numan, AC/DC, Kiss, T. Rex…. We've all played different kinds of music over the years. Red Hare has the chassis of a hardcore/rock band, but I'd happily pepper in anything in that we think sounds good.

Shawn: I don't really think about it that deeply. I just listen to the songs you (Jason) present me. Seriously. I mean, maybe you heard reggae when you were seven, or the Cars when you were fourteen, and that's all creeping in now with the songs you write, but I don't think it's a conscious thing. It happens organically. You play what you think sounds good, or what you think fits the song—after it's done you can point at different bits and say, "That's new wave," or, "That's AC/DC residue."

Jason, your obsessive and sometimes costly detail/packaging is intense: the early comics of Swiz, the sheer, sleek modernism of Bluetip and Retisonic, "a synthesis of Reid Miles blue-note sophistication/simplicity with a Jetsons-like mid-sixties futurism" you admitted, or the new Red Hare hybrid style of natural imagery, careful craft, and horror design— those red eyes in the liner notes look like a color-saturated 1970s horror film! Did this happen as an evolution or stem from Dischord design or sources elsewhere?

Jason: I've done hundreds of record covers over the years for many different bands, drifting in and out of styles and approaches. In that time, I've been heavily involved in the design side of all the releases I've played on, too. Swiz, Bluetip, and Retisonic releases have the aesthetic through-line you described. But when Dave's friend Adam Jones offered to do the artwork for Red Hare's first album, I saw it as a chance to step back from putting my stink on yet another album. Like Adam's work with Tool (*10,000 Days*), the rabbits he drew for the Red Hare cover were amazing: beautifully creepy, quite a departure from my Jetson's/Bluenote send-ups. I put Adam's art into a package, pairing it with somewhat creepy close-up eye photos, but naturally colored to counter the scary/gory vibe of the cover. Adam kept pushing me to go all the way, embracing the horror with a red wash across the faces. Glad I took his advice.

Red Hare by N. Darmrong

Red Hare by N. Darmrong

SWIZ

TWELVE INCH
A V A I L A B L E   N O W
$IX UNITED post paid $EVEN CANADA
sammich records p.o. box 32292 wash DC 20007

AMERICANADIAN TYPE TOUR

JULY   AUGUST   '89
with american standard (some)

SWIZ

Supertouch
with: BURN, TCO, & EDGEWISE

Sunday February 18, 1990 3pm
club pizzazz 2
6th & girard
NOTE NEW ADDRESS·ALL AGES WELCOME
FOR MORE INFO CALL (215) 524-9133 BRIAN
A SNAPPERHEAD PRODUCTION

concierto
Pero esta vez si que es. En serio!!!
domingo 20 agosto
mundo paralelo
torrelavega
hora: 21.30 h.
gratis!!!!!

Bluetip
dischord rcs.
washington DC

Bruising, skywards thrusting, guitar soaked songs
from these compadres of FUGAZI.
cHEAP sWEATY fUN 248

BLUETIP

DISCHORD records

Holy Shit! It's the return of....
FISH TAKE

Upside down beats and fuzzed-out acoustics from this rising Bristol band.

Chikinki

MON. APRIL 9th

Tickets : £5.00 (Rockaway) : £6.00 (Door)

TJ'S NIGHTCLUB
CLARENCE PLACE, NEWPORT
SOUTH WALES, NP9 0NE
TEL: 01633 216608

TJ'S
www.tjs-newport.demon.co.uk

Tickets from:
ROCKAWAY RECORDS
PUGHSTONE MARKET
NEWPORT, NP2 1BD

KEROSENE 454

Silver Spring, MD

DISCHORD records

BLUE ▽ TIP

DISCHORD

JEUDI 9 OCTOBRE

PEZNER

at the centre
donegall st
belfast
from washington d.c
on dischord records
3rd time out
with support
the redneck manifesto
from dublin
& **the kabinboy**
from belfast

bluetip

12.11.99

2030 £3.50

PEZNER / VENDREDI 5/3

BLUE TIP

DISCHORD

FROM WASHINGTON, D.C

w/ THE FAREWELL BEND & AINA

AT THE DRIVE IN

LiVE!!!!!

With!!!

BLUETIP

and Lassie...

BLOOD PARTY

and...

LIVE!
Friday,
August 20th
@ CD Merchant
1517 W Main, Boise
7pm $5

for info:
331-1200

Reviews

Moss Icon - Complete Discography, Temporary Residence

Retisonic - Robots Fucking, Arctic Rodeo Recordings

Originally published by Popmatters in 2012.

Two album releases this spring highlight the primal potency and gritty glory of two East Coast musical institutions that have remained off-the-radar far too long. They include the obscure late 1980's animistic art-punk of Moss Icon, from Annapolis, Maryland, and the continued efforts of Jason Farrell, the music maker-cum-graphic designer, originally from Washington D.C., who has forged over three decades worth of complex, edgy, and fecund power-punk that has defined what is best about infiltrating and recasting genres.

In the late 1980s, Moss Icon erupted in the wake of post-hardcore, when hyper-fast templates wore thin and bands kept their gruff, choleric blasts but chose to slow down the backbeats into territory more aligned with Flipper. That is the kind of slow, knife-edge chaos evoked in "I'm Back Sleeping, Or Fucking, Or Something" and "Divinity Cove," found on the new and rather pedestrian titled Compete Discography. With shambolic spoken word messiness, the trembling tunes feel equal parts ominous and penetrating, like dark etudes for a rust-eaten world.

Like early Shudder to Think, Fugazi, and Lungfish, Moss Icon tapped into punk's ethos of experimentation without forsaking its punch and putsch quality: punk meant to deliver tough goods, not froth, and aimed to topple the status quo of rock, not to become just another satellite of alternative culture, safely sanitized. Punks didn't want to go beyond the illusion of music capitalism, it seemed, they wanted to scratch and hack at it until that illusion tattered. In the wake of such dismantling came the music of emotional liberation and a genre made from blood and guts, not plastic.

Moss Icon beckons listeners to the time-warp cauldron when "emo" had not become a hollow cliché for marketing purposes, a time when post-hardcore hadn't splintered into a million sub-groupings. Their body of work seems to scowl at the herding instinct and remind listeners that boredom should not easily commence.

"Lyburnum" grinds and pulses in roiling drum cacophony as meditative vocals evoke funereal "dead lilies." Listening closely, one can detect hints of early New Order, circa 1981. Some songs, though, do tumble in unscrewed manic beats, like "Cricketty Rise," but those conversational style vocals (hmm, perhaps a nod to Lou Reed, Suicide, and Leonard Cohen) still anchor the pliant songs.

By the time tunes like "Kick the Can" were released, the band's production values were amped up and the dense, free form poem-as-lyrics more nuanced within the mix. The fluid and ever-changing "Memorial," with its humanitarian portrayal of hunger's link to government legislation, takes up a rancorous rock'roll edge in places, only to subdue itself back in percussive pointillism. Imagine late-period Crass mixed with Americana shades.

Some songs burn with phosphorescent glare, including "Hate in Me." Its furious analysis of love/hate dichotomies sears the spinal column. "What They Lack" is equally poignant. The lyrical plea for "please don't forget me" seems to act like a corollary to Husker Du's combustible tune "I'll Never Forget You" (1984). It also acts as the album's final inscription, with more than a tad bit of irony. The public bootlegged and swapped files of the band until a company like Temporary Residence kicked into gear, making Moss Icon a genuine catalog presence. The label patched the holes in indie music history.

In turn, Jason Farrell is a mythic figure that few people seem to pinpoint when discussing the legacy of Dischord Records, the label for whom he produced manifold album designs, including the post-modern packaging of bands like Fugazi. While Farrell undoubtedly contributed to the aesthetics of that generation, he also made sizzling records in bands like Swiz, whose brash late-hardcore prowess injected some bile back into Washington D.C.'s sometimes laconic late-1980's music breeds.

As a young gun, Farrell melded the sizable crunch of early Discharge with the frenetic unhinged dynamism of The Damned. Tunes like the under-produced "Time" and "Lie" blistered in frenzied, emotive, and inchoate onslaughts, helped by the cranky vocals of Shawn Brown, whose bark on tunes like "Taste" and "Stone" scrapes like sandpaper. Meanwhile, tunes like "Sunstroke" laid the groundwork for post-hardcore icons Quicksand and Snapcase.

As that band imploded, Farrell continued to design packaging and form bands like Fury and Sweetbelly Freakdown, which merited some attention. Once he emerged as singer/guitarist in the rock'n'roll inflected Bluetip, audiences truly awakened to his uber-underground talents. Bluetip was like telling Farrell, "ready steady go." Four albums later, the work stands as testament to his ability to dispatch songs with seemingly easy panache by merging hardcore's neurons with smart rock'n'roll embellishments. Thus, the catalog is seminal, a nod to procreative urges.

Yet, the prized possession of Farrell may actually be the mid-2000s gestated Retisonic, a three-headed talent pool that combines Farrell's most nimble pop-mindedness with the gymnastic drumming of Joe Gorelick, which is kept in check by the throbbing bass plumbed by Jim Gimball. Their greatest slab, Return to Me has languished in a no man's land of small distributors, like the French label Modern City. The 2004 material was a gem filtering Farrell's past and present with uncanny skill sets. Tiny hints of Bay City Rollers, Gary Numan, B-52s, and yes, some Discharge and Minor Threat, were tucked effortlessly into the folds of the redoubtable album.

Robots Fucking, which was recorded during a 2005-2006 time table, revisits this tempestuous territory with only slightly less robust production. "Wait … Lookout!" takes aim at self-control, issuing fine observations with driving beats and hallmark guitar riffage. "Airtight" pounces with a similar tempo, though with some start and stop punctures and dizzying drums. By debating themes like "blank life" and "living airtight," the song marks volatile territory between fortitude and feebleness.

The pounding "Necropolitan" is a slab of poetic witnessing. The narrator, or the public, for which the narrator is a surrogate, suffers an overdose of "distractions/movie stars/sports teams" and "blind faith in technology, religion, and nationality." The tune is damning and denunciating, relevant and riling.

A few Swiz guitarisms surface on the power-pop with metal-edge "High on Denial," which loosens up with a few handclaps, melodic urges, and ambient spoken-word cuts that inhabit the distorted blitz. The ender, "Defined," comes on slow and sweet, with dimpled piano, layered and gauzy vocals, ample assonance ("you can back track bones to birthdays"), and swaying swan song rhythms.

Both Farrell's Retisonic and Moss Icon prove that worthy music sometimes take years to surface, or re-appear in full-fledged forms, even as bands muster legendary status in the digital era, in which everything is usually available instantly.

Hopefully, both these releases will not simply annotate the careers of each nor simply provide fetish fulfillment for those seeking albums and CDs, not another downloaded file.

Neither band feels worn out, treading in water, or run-of-the-mill. Instead, they provide a glimpse of unseen powers. Acting as cornerstone -- not cursory -- music, each is exultant, acting like a spell that does not obey sell-by dates.

Additional Reviews

Alternative version previously published on Left of the Dial's defunct website as well as Popmatters.

Deathfix - Self-titled, Dischord Records

Although billed as a return to the daze/days of glam rock by the likes of drum connoisseur Brendan Canty (of Fugazi fame, now switched to guitar and vocals) and cohorts from Morel, Faraquet, and Medications, this is no simple stab at early 1970's teen beat glitter romp ala Slade or the darker, art-infused hubris of David Bowie and Roxy Music. Instead, imagine a wider, less self-conscious territory that feels equally at home with expansive textures fit for a Tricky tune as well as lyrical twists common in Fugazi music. Some songs seem merely like a restless, spoken-word homage to cultural heroes like Salvador Dali, Kanye West, and Marianne Faithful ("Dali's House," which echoes the style of Wolfgang Press' banter), others feel like languid, harmonizing, and spirited pop jams veering into cosmic slop ("Transmission"), while still others feel like short stories wielding indie rock slyness ("Hospital"). Deathfix, above all, feels post-genre, or like an endless genre mash-up that rejects simple cold cut bricolage; instead, listeners succumb to a molten, groove-based, and murky modus operandi unafraid of tampering with the formulas of Raspberries-meets-Spiritualized, gleaned with punk smarts.

The Evens - The Odds, Dischord Records

The Evens, featuring guitarist Ian MacKaye and spouse, drummer Amy Farina, know that less is more. As a co-singing duo inhabiting a gender gray zone, they eschew garage rock bombast, facile indie rock pretense, and processed pomp. Instead, as the muted cousin of Fugazi, which MacKaye helmed for two decades, their appeal is found within reserved tendencies. They replace the emotional cliff-hangers and dissonant dexterity of that band with domicile (un)rock, even include house lamps on their stage. The nasally MacKaye maintains a kitchen sink style, wielding unfussy rhythmic thrusts that dance with Farina's incessant, propulsive grooves and her stark voice, echoing a bit of P.J. Harvey. Cadences found in the mesmerizing "King of Kings" unfurl at the speed of Lungfish and reveal wry wordplay and alliteration. Meanwhile, "Wanted Criminals" approximates an avid social critique, decrying an age of hive-mind surveillance, while "Warble Factor - Version" and "Let's Get Well" mine the existential tension between nature -- life and dying -- and fakery: media concoctions of beauty and finance. Recalling Samuel Becket's sense of endlessly re-worked language, the band reminds listeners that intelligence is not measured by hype but by exploring the road less traveled.

Artificial Peace - Complete Session, Dischord Records

Although some of these tracks have been available previously, like the seminal compilation *Flex Your Head*, this newly re-mastered early 1980s harDCore is a flagrant gem of youth-driven uber fury. For scraped, ratty-sounding but intelligent vocals, a defoliated and dizzying blend of musical crunch and brief melody, check out "Suburban Wasteland," their East Coast version of Circle Jerks' bitingly satirical "Beverly Hills." Much of this aggressive aggregation clocks in under two minutes and competes with brethren bands Void and Faith for finely-etched, breathless anomie that attacks war, shitty DJs, and materialism. They even take The Troggs "Wild Thing" for a beat-on-the-brat ride.

Dag Nasty - Dag with Shawn, Dischord Records

By the mid-1980s, hardcore seemed to stall into warty, same-samey style or mired in rock'n'roll ambitions, like TSOL and Black Flag. Then Dag Nasty, a Washington D.C . smorgasbord featuring Bostonian straight-edge crooner Dave Smalley on vocals, shot from the genre gate with dizzying, melodic, emo-ish intensity that reignited a generation. Original singer Shawn Brown, caught in these well-produced demos before he jettisoned, offers blistering, bellowing, and incendiary vocal stabs for the cherished tunes. Critics argue Smalley added too much sheen, so these tracks capture Dag Nasty sans lube and oil, in their grittier glory.

Government Issue - Boycott Stabb Complete Session, Dischord Records

Sure, Dr. Strange released G.I discographies containing this pitch perfect nimble speed-punk but Dischord offers both the original album as-is, plus a series of previously unmixed and rare tracks left in obscurity. Singer John Stabb refused to play the punk rock game. Known to wear lengthy tube socks or 1970s thrift store duds, his sardonic vocals and quick wit (partially borrowed from fave bands like the Damned) are in splendid bursting-haiku form here. With bracing guitar from Brian Baker (Minor Threat), the band eviscerates annoyingly happy people, fashionites, religious rip-offs, and useless new wavers, all woven into lightning-break songs defining hardcore as an alternative to jock-anthems for the buzzed hair crews.

Red Hare - Nites of Midnite, Dischord Records

Featuring the core members of Swiz, the post-hardcore Washington D.C. band that bridged the 1980s-1990s with their tough-as-nails attitude, infectiously sing-along refrains, and nimble and voracious musical outpourings, this project reveals the ageless angst that can still seize the night, especially when one enters middle-age doldrums. Irascible singer Shawn Brown, who first famously poured his viral vitriol onto crowds in blazing Dag Nasty, and combustible, insatiable guitarist Jason Farrell (Bluetip, Retisonic) join dizzying drummer Joe Gorelick (Garden Variety, Bluetip, Retisonic) and Swiz regular Dave Eight to shred all notions of retiring their chops and atavism. Dischord has not offered something as acerbic ("Fuck Your Career!"), acrid, and bitterly anthemic ("Be Half," "Dialed In"), minus their abundant and admirable re-issues of the likes of Government Issue and the Faith, in well over twenty years. Yes, these same Swiz veterans tried something similar in Sweatbelly Freakdown, their mid-1990's project, but that effort felt a tad uninspired; whereas, this album blasts from the gates with teeth bared, replete with Farrell's sideways nod to mutant metal licks, Gorelick's effortless percussive punches, and Brown's steely street poetry on steroids. If this doesn't leave an ex-hardcore listener breathless, renewed, and invigorated, then he or she should return to a heap of retrograde vinyl platters and ignore the future. As the final, pummeling, bass heavy tune "Nites of Midnite" (with Farrell dropping in for vocal) attests, it's time for people to take off their costumes, believe in whatever, run naked through their fears, and start living again. Swiz is dead: long live fiercely focused Red Hare.

Lungfish – A.C.R. 1999, Dischord Records

14 May 2012

Having melded a curious and compelling sound during the post-hardcore halcyon days of the late 1980s in the Washington D.C. – Maryland nexus, Lungfish proved that stamina and resilience, and sticking to artistic prowess, can create a fertile legacy that bends the rules. Rather than always innovate and paving new paths every few years, Lungfish stayed on course, cutting records with consistent mystique, murkiness, and mantra-like quality.

This material is an artifact from fine de siecle 1999, a previously unreleased testament to Craig Bowen, who twisted the knobs at A.C.R studios in Baltimore. The band didn't stop to release them. In fact, they plowed ahead, forging new songs, ultimately re-recording several A.C.R. tracks at iconic Inner Ear Studios, which handled dozens of Dischord bands. So, while this album doesn't present a bevy of virgin material, it does present a unique twist to the path of these songs – a glimpse into their original birth chamber.

Lungfish is not the type of band, like Fugazi, that seemed atomized and atavistic during every turn of phrase, emoting a lexicon of anguish, personal politics, and art. Instead, Lungfish appeared to be a band tethered to fluid restraint, control, ambience, and roiling but paced rhythms. They were the dizzying pause in the storm, but retained the storm's heavy signature.

Once, when opening for hectic Brainiac in New York City during the Ohio band's zenith, Lungfish took the stage with almost immobile gestures. The drummer faced his amp most of the set, as if listening to his own shadow, while singer-cum-artist Daniel Higgs cut an imposing figure of a wayward seafarer, tattoo collector, handyman, and visionary homeless man. While Brainiac was marked by impulse, mayhem, and the body electric, Lungfish seemed like an exorcism in slow motion, a wailing soliloquy leaking into the club's ambience.

This album's opener "Eternal Nightfall" feels like ice melting: the pump of the bass drum and the dribbling guitar meet in a groove that is softly locked. Meanwhile, both "Symbiosis" and "Screams of Joy" feel as lyrically taut and terse as an early Ezra Pound poem, yet the mutating vocals, for which Higgs is a legend, feel both cryptically religious ("The Christ is suckled") and coldly observant as imagism ("screams of joy/ can be heard/ within the perimeter / of our open air facility).

On one hand, the band seems to operate effortlessly within the traditions of Killing Joke (sonic repetition, opaque and cryptic lyrics, primordial spirituality) and poetic variations that range from direct presentation of life data to obtuse, meandering thought-spiels spelling out lines like, "The brittle skin/ of embalmed limbs / declares a polynym." Found on the tune, "I Will Walk Between You," such phrasing feels fecundly formal. Higgs' nimble wit, assonance, surrealism, and effortless play with the textures of language amount to a powerful modus operandi.

Sure, some will suggest Lungfish seems stuck in time and tempo, each song evoking a sort of redux, a revisitation of each other, like an elongated, multi-volume sequence sometimes frustratingly knit together in a cocoon. Yet, that is akin to calling AC/DC repetitious and redundant. Instead, I imagine Lungfish as plumbing the depths of a larger oral poetics, in which purposeful, poignant songs arc into each other, forming cycles grappling with birth, life, and death in each stanza.

In fact, the songs become an index of being – the soundtrack of living in a riling world as connected to folkloric rites as it is to the video age. On "Sex War," which evokes the body's trials and tribulations, Higgs fittingly belts out, "Until the repetitions cease / The repetition must increase." Such song maps life's patterns and permutations, from flesh-based anxieties to metaphysical and lexical flux.

One does not have to ponder so hard to enjoy tunes like "Shapes in Space." The cosmic drift of the song seems indebted to Roky Erickson's lysergic repertoire. Equally profound and slightly danceable, it nods to the outer limits (space, time) and inner limits (skulls, breasts), and the passageways in-between.

Those that prefer songs to languish in Pop and rest in empty shells of clichés might choose meat other than Lungfish. For those that seek songs doubling as abstract verbal sculpture or wayward scripture, Lungfish is a vendor of those vibes.

By Malcolm Rivera

I Am Subject to Change! An Interview with Alec MacKaye of The Faith, Ignition and The Warmers

Originally published by Popmatters, 2011.

Years ago, the lore of Dischord and Washington D.C. area punk filtered down into the vocabulary of a worldwide audience that avidly locked onto terms like straight-edge and emo, both slang and now genre, that stemmed from a clustered scene jolting the music world in the early years of the 1980s. The Faith were a bit of both: a gritty, nuanced 'heartcore' punk band with succinct, potent lyrics that emoted irascible punk sentiments long before both emo became just another overplayed youth brand.

This collection combines both demos recorded prior to their split LP with Void and a re-issue of their superb *Subject to Change* EP, coveted by fans, enthusiasts, and critics as a bedrock slab of Washington D.C. hardcore, promulgated as harDCore. To this end, people routinely point out that singer Alec MacKaye's trademark warbly howl is often overlooked in favor of another MacKaye – brother Ian, the scorched-voiced singer for Minor Threat.

Minor Threat's barreling tunes invoked everything from incisive punk placards ("Stand Up and Be Counted"), re-imagined and retrofitted rock'n'roll classics ("Steppin' Stone," "Sometimes Good Guys Don't Wear White"), unbottled rage ("Seeing Red" "Screaming at a Wall") and self-referential irony ("Minor Threat" "Cashing In"). The Faith's tunes, not quite as nimble, but equally ferocious, feature a more plaintive (hence, the emo tag) side of punk's lyrical underbelly, condensed into under two-minute songs that feel like a blast furnace.

Replete with the murky, layered, and twin-powered hypnotic guitar crunch of Michael Hampton and Eddie Janney, which feels blistery the remastered *Subject to Change* tracks amount to high-marks in East Coast underground music history. While "Aware" and "Say No More" are a bit slower (ala the speed of U.K. Subs) than typical cookie cutter hardcore mania circa 1983, they prove that mood, syncopation, raw harmonies, build-ups, and taut terseness can congeal into pithy forms.

Meanwhile, in lines from "Say No More," MacKaye leans into the listener's bald ear, invoking pleas for common sense humanity (how you treat me / is how I treat you ... the blame lies within). The hand claps at the end deliver a surprise, like a nod to pop in the middle of shrapnel.

Sure, blitzkrieg tunes also burst here and there across the album, like the tensely coiled "Limitations" and "No Choice," both of which rail against conventions and limitations ("what kind of world is this?") that compel people to conform against their will. Freedom is at stake, and each line of the songs probes that problem with heated diligence, including people's tendency to make excuses.

For years, however, my favorite has been the tender explosity of "Untitled" ("the feeling's real, but it's untitled"), which really explains all the moments when words escape my tongue, especially as my body is flushed with feeling. Sometimes words fail, MacKaye intones in haiku-like precision.

Then title track "Subject to Change" sets the tone of the debate. Punk should not box in, categorize, or force people to suffer some tunnel vision precepts. Punk is about adapting, changing, and shifting, allowing flexibility and freedom, not orthodoxy ("subject to change what I say ... subject to change what I do ... and so are you"). MacKaye resembles a tradition-bearer carrying forward the dictum of Walt Whitman, who exclaimed, "I contain multitudes." MacKaye further explored this, intelligently, by forging bands like Ignition and The Warmers, who expanded the definition and style of punk while sometimes incurring harsh judgment from purists.

The Faith demo tracks, precursors to the band's split LP with Void, reveal tracks that are slightly rougher and rawer replicas of their previously released counterparts, down to the very exact length, give or take a few seconds. Don't expect any longer takes, unearthed guitar solos, impromptu jams, or studio gibber jabber, like the material discovered for the Government Issue re-issues last year. Still, they emit poignancy and power. More importantly, a different version of "In the Black" pops up. This tune links the band to earlier Britpunk tendencies and locals like Black Market Baby, as does the opener "It's Time."

While fakers and pretenders will still shrug off the band, and many fans will desire more than just rehashed old catalog tracks (where are the live tracks? basement tapes?), the quality of the re-mastering and packaging will at least sate some people, like me, who yearn for a hardcore punk era that seems more authentic, spirited, and community-oriented than the current digital dynasty.

When working on the release of The Faith demos, did anything about the material surprise you?

The only work I did was to listen to, and okay the mix. No surprises, really. I have actually listened to that stuff on a semi-regular basis over the years. I thought it held up pretty well, though, and with a new mix, sounded great.

As a teenage punk, did you feel any affinity with older local bands like the Slickee Boys, 9353, and Tru Fax and the Insaniacs?

I was in a few bands during my teenage years. When I was 14, I definitely felt encouraged by Slickee Boys and Tru Fax. I liked going to see them play, and was excited when I saw Kim Kane at Untouchables shows or when Diana Quinn asked us to open for them on a couple of gigs. Tru Fax even bailed on a show once, when the club wouldn't let us (The Untouchables) play – because we were too young. As I recall, when the manager said we couldn't go on, Diana said, "If they're not playing – we're not playing!" as sort of a threat, since they were the headline act. The manager of the club just said, "Okay. Then you're not playing either." So, they took a hit for us – pretty cool. By the time Faith started playing, there was a little distance, I suppose. We were heading into a more intense, less carefree, or quirky kind of approach to music, than the Slickees or Tru Fax. Our audiences were different than theirs, our music was different, even our intent was different.

I think those "older" bands recognized, somewhat, the conventional rock approach and worked within its framework more than we did, even if it was not straight up rock-biz stuff. The Untouchables and Faith, and other bands like us, completely ignored the music industry. In fact, we worked in spite of, and in many ways, against it. So, philosophically, there was some distance. I always liked those bands and the people in them, though! 9353 were not an older band -- they were around when I was in my twenties. They were interesting and pushed an envelope, but they weren't part of my formation, per se. I was pretty friendly with them, if that's what you mean, though.

In the mid-1990s, you said, "There's the core in the middle of punk that I trust and it protects itself from invading whatevers and it's still pure and still great." What do you think invaded punk, and what do you believe is pure still?

I think it was invaded by lazy, exuberant capitalism. People seeing punk shows as fish barrels (as in: easy as shooting fish in a barrel). And I don't just mean, abstract, withery over-lords trying to control the youth revolution. I also mean young, peppy people deciding that it would be a perfect blend of their interests if they apply their new knowledge of entertainment law, or what they learned during their summer internship at Columbia Records to their own scene. I see bands now that look like they are performing a soundtrack for their merch table. And they beg people to buy their stuff right there on stage. I suppose it must be done -- but I like when bands just get up there and destroy, then leave. If I want their record or shirt or keyfob, I'll buy it!

Yes, I think there still exists an incorruptible core. It's the place where all the stuff comes from and it comes with such force that contaminants can't work backwards against it, they can only feed from it later.

You summed up punk's credos, arguing that it always represented a "challenge to mediocrity." When making music with the Untouchables and The Faith, what mediocrity were you challenging?

I guess punk did its job well if we have already forgotten what sorts of mediocrity is out there. I meant the mediocrity of people being intellectually and creatively lazy, when they can work harder. Its not enough to simply take risks or be iconoclastic, one should stay true to and work hard at the things that inspire them, especially if it is marginal. Mediocrity is when you give up on that. If you relax too much, it sounds like you're just alright with everything and, well, that's just alright...-- I think its better to reach deeper.

"A lot of people ... rely on Dischord to be it's own equitable and personable entity," you surmised on *Diskant.net*. As the marketplace frays and consumer-producer relationships change in the digital era, how do you think Dischord maintains these traits? I remember the handwritten letters fondly.

I can't recall saying that - but I agree with it. I would say that Dischord has performed that task and still lives there. Its consistency is radical. It has remained reliable and dedicated to the people that buy Dischord Records, as well as to the people that make Dischord Records. If Dischord had let up or given up completely, you would not be sending me this interview. *Subject To Change* might have happened, but it would not likely have the same relevance. That's a quality that is worth more than one-time money by a factor of ten, at least ... Dischord still offers the thing it offered before -- which is all that it takes to maintain something.

An iconic picture of you graces Teen Idles' "Minor Disturbance," EP - crossed, studded arms, and Xs drawn on the back of your hands. How important, do you feel, is visual culture to the legacy of punk? Do record art and flyers feel as potent to you as the music?

In the hands of Crass and some other bands, album and flyer art is as potent as the music. In all bands, it is an opportunity to be more creative - unless you want to make a statement by not saying anything. A lot of bands just want to get a record out and not worry about the wrapper.

Some people really just want the music to speak for itself, and don't want anyone "reading the book by its cover," so I can see not wanting to over-invest in album art. But when I think of my own relationship to records as a kid - I don't think I thumb-tacked any plain white record covers on my wall. I didn't prop them up and stare at them while listening to music through headphones, the way I did with other records whose album art I can remember right now.

The legacy of punk... the "punk" visual aesthetic has permeated everything these days. I don't know what to make of it - it reminds me of *A Clockwork Orange*. In the movie version, there are grandmas wearing leather jackets and dying their hair crazy colors because it is simply the fashion of the day.

From the outside, the D.C. area's music scene always felt very integrated and pluralistic, from Red C to Void to Beefeater and Swiz. Yet, people remind me that it took root in a majority-black city, so it was less diverse than it seems. Looking back, would you describe the scene as diverse?

I don't think I can say with any certainty how diverse the scene was or was not, concerning the ratio of the city's population. Perhaps in comparison to other scenes in cities that had similar racial statistics, the D.C. scene was more diverse ... maybe less. I'm sure there is some kid out there, crunching numbers for his or her dissertation on this very topic, right now.

When I was a kid, moving through it, I was not counting heads and profiling, worrying about ensuring that all ethnicities were proportionately represented, according to the most recent census. I think it is safe to say that, though it was not exactly Hardcore DeGrassi High, there was some mixing it up.

Some argue the straight-edge scene was a close-minded, dumb adolescent scene. Do you believe straight-edge offered some useful core values?

I can only speak for myself when I say that "straightedge" was for me, at that time, not as much of a scene (the lyric sheet should have had quote marks on the word "scene" to indicate sarcasm we didn't know we would have to be explaining it in decades to come!) as it was a reaction to a tired sort of nihilism that was not going to serve me/us well. Drinking cheap beer and fighting over nothing was too time consuming, at the very least. I had energy and wanted to get things done and not step in someone else's quicksand along the way.

Young people pursuing things with an unclouded mind is not the worst way to start out, I'd say. The vagaries of life will destroy them soon enough – why make it easy on the destroyer.

The Faith wrote mostly about personal politics. Ignition seemed to enlarge the lyrical and musical terrain, especially on songs like "Lucky Thirteen." What led you in that direction?

We were pretty young when we were in The Faith, still in high school. What was happening to us directly was the most important thing to us. By the time we were in Ignition – we were old enough to be drafted, drive cars and influence policy by voting, if we were so inclined.
Driving around in a van, seeing the world, talking to people in other places, listening to more music, will enlarge your view...

Ignition's visual material – album, CDs, 45 singles, and flyers – seem to appropriate or resemble many non-Western aesthetics. Was that a very deliberate decision?

The two Chris' did almost all the artwork, so I can't speak at length about it – but I don't think there was a particular push towards non-western motifs.

The Warmers feels like a perfect meld between the thrust, wordplay, and experimentation of early punk with power trio tension. Did playing with the band satisfy you on the same level as The Faith? The Warmers feels equally inchoate and fresh to me.
Glad that the Warmers felt perfect. And yes, it was as satisfying as anything I have ever done. And it was a decidedly imperfect band – by design.

Recently, you noted, "The small Hiroshige show we had at the Philip's Collection a few years back changed the way I dream." Could you explain the effects of the 19th century Japanese ukiyo-e artist a bit more?

It was merely a statement of fact. After looking closely at the Tokaido Road series, I had dreams that were unlike any I could remember. I don't need to know what that means, it just happened.

When making your own art, like drawing in pencil, you sometimes listen to Library of Congress field recordings, punk rock, or dub reggae. What links the three – authenticity, vividness, and topicality?

That was easy, you just answered the question for me! Yes on all three.

Like Jeff Nelson, you enjoy collecting items, albeit with very different tastes, like "bonsai trees, model cars, stopped clocks, and old padlocks and other metal things, ruined paint brushes, hardware clad in naturally acquired patination . . ." as the Philip Collection blog recounted. What draws you to these items – the folklore of the industrial age?

That was a partially sarcastic answer. "Naturally acquired patination" is art-speak for rust. I like old things of high quality and durability. Even if some old thing don't "work," they remind me of what it used to be like, when things could be repaired mechanically or were fabricated from quality materials. Now our best things are made from cheap plastic, which is apparently good enough.

Faith By Tiffany Pruitt

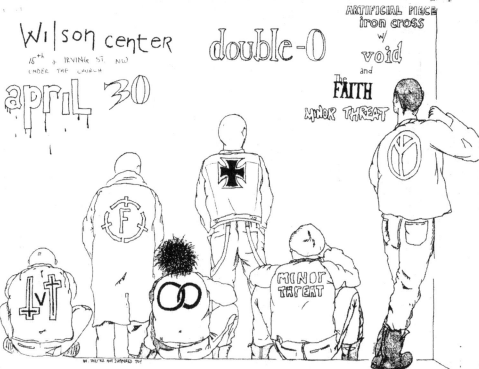

Wilson center
15th & IRVING ST. NW
UNDER THE CHURCH

april 30

double-0

ARTIFICIAL PIECE
iron cross
w/
void
and
The FAITH
MINOR THREAT

hornets

Iron Cross

FAITH ✡

1844 ONTARIO PL.
Time 4:00 PM to 7:00 PM
ADMISSION $4.00

MATINEE
Tomorrow   4:00 O'clock

B.E.R. Production

DISCHORD records

SUBJECT TO CHANGE

FAITH

ON SALE AT

Record & Tape Ltd.
Kemp Mill Records
Record & Tape Exchange
Melody Record Shop
Joe's Record Paradise
AND, OF COURSE,
Yesterday & Today Records

VOID
DOUBLE-O
minor threat
COMMON CAUSE
IRON CROSS
THE FAITH
APRIL
30
AT THE
Wilson
Center
15TH & IRVING ST.

Cheryl Eve Bayer, winner of more than 165 beauty pageant awards. "Some people have stamp collections. Well, I have a trophy colle...

IRON CROSS
The Faith
Double-O
Black Flag
The Effigies from Chicago

Sept. 17
at the wilson center
15th and IRVING St. N.W. WASHINGTON D.C.
7:00

I Am the Tempest - Chris Thomson

Originally published by Left of the Dial website.

David, thanks for your interest and questions. I just wanted to throw a bit of a preface at you cause I think it needs to be said.

I seem to find myself in this strange role, not to my making. I just kind of feel that people have a relationship with my music but certainly not with me. They discover the records, CD's long after they came out, and I think it gives people a distorted view of life and times of these bands and certainly of me as well. It's not that this music existed in some vacuum. We toured, we played out, and we did our best to make the performances accessible. So, if you're upset you never got to see Monorchid or Circus Lupus, I really don't give a shit, there were plenty of opportunities. And while I'm at it, I'd like to extend a gigantic steaming fuck you to Brian Lovitt who re-pressed the "Let them Eat" record when he was specifically agreed not too, and while it might not be a lot of money, he has yet to share the profits with the band.

You moved to Chicago not too long ago (three years, now?) and have mentioned that a host of D.C. expats live there too. Beyond offering a good place to work, why has Chicago been such an "easy fit" compared to D.C., which you recently (2003) described as much more "serious" in terms of music? Is that to say that the Bloodshot and Touch and Go folks are more laid back?

I've been in Chicago a little over two years. I haven't lived in D.C. since 1999. Chicago reminds me to a certain extent of a gigantic D.C. with its residential neighborhoods, similar ethnic mix, and blending of rich and poor. I don't know if the labels have anything to do with the music scene. T&G doesn't have any Chicago bands on their label--well Shellac-- but I can't think of anyone else. It feels like Bloodshot is trying to foster more of a community, but I'm certainly not an expert. But honestly, there's just so many people doing music here--all kinds, not just indie/ punk rock etc. Chicago is this Mecca, so if you grow up in Ohio or Missouri, you kind of gravitate here. It's relatively cheap to live here, which is probably the biggest factor. There are a ton of places to play. I think the Fireside Bowl has a lot to do with fostering the music scene. For ten years, all these kids have had their musical education through the Fireside, maybe even their first chance to play. They get older, listen to different music, and return as Empty Bottle hipsters.

By the way, did you, or was it other members of Circus Lupus, that lived for awhile in Madison, WI (land of Killdozer, Tar Babies, and Mecht Mensch), where the first single was published?

I used to see Bill, the drummer of Killdozer, all the time. He worked in a record store I visited on a regular basis. At that point, the Tar Babies were perusing a Red Hot Chili Peppers vibe. On one of Circus Lupus' first tours we played in Pittsburgh, this kid Brian was starting this little label, Cubist Productions. He offered to put out a single by us.

While in the Monorchid, you said, D.C. "has succumbed to the panacea of formulae. There is a formula for everything. Bands, music, record labels, people are motivated not so much by what they feel but by an array of formulas created to save time, money, lessen emotional involvement, and ensure so-called 'success.' What happens is, all the bands sound alike, and everyone is chasing the same major-label dream—a dream that has in fact disappointed all of our regional subscribers." Was that simply a

way to sell the Monorchird, or was it a genuine criticism of stagnation and conformity endemic to the D.C. area?

To a certain extent, it's a lot of piss and vinegar. But at the same time, I think I was bummed out at the vibe of the music scene. It was during this period when I can't tell you how many friends and people I had played with who were like, "We're going to sign, we're going to make it. It's going to work out for us." Because I've always been in these weird bands that don't really roll off the ears all that easily, we'd go on the road traveling with people we thought were our friends and you get subjected to all this bullshit. Everyone was acting out his/her rock'n'roll fantasy, like bands were talking about their recipe for success, "Who's your booking agent? Who's your publicist?" Suddenly, people were running their bands like corporations. It led to a lot of disappointment and the sad realization that we are not all in this together. It just got to be lame when you are playing with a band you think you are friends with and they are looking you in the face and telling you that they are more important and valuable than you, so you get $75 from the door, but they'll take $300. So, I just felt like a prop that was rented out for other people's credibility.

Years ago, when Circus Lupus was in its heyday, the DC/Chicago connection seemed most visible with things like the Trenchmouth/Lupus split 7". Yet, you are now on GSL, a California label. Do think there still exists regional differences, like style and sensibility, or do you think that Sonny from GSL and you could easily have come from Tampa Bay or any other place?

There was and is still differences between scenes, but then there seem to be waves, like when the Make Up tours and a year later everyone from Sioux Falls to Birmingham is wearing suits or white belts. The differences between scenes and locales were more obvious in the past. Today, between the Internet, media, and wave of chain stores and restaurants, a lot of the country is looking, eating, and dressing the same. But it's not like this is a new development, for there have always been bands who kind of pop up out of nowhere and travel, bringing their own reinterpretation of punk and their own style. Then, suddenly, kids in Birmingham, Dayton, and Lubbock are dressing differently, wearing white belts or trucker wallets, or growing beards and toying with synthesizers. I think it's that "Kids-from-the-big-city must know what's cool kind of thing." So, pollination has always been there, but today it happens a lot faster. Because Sonny and I are still, after all these years and after all these bands, still playing punk music and traveling in our punk circles while so many of our peers have moved on to other things, I would say that Sonny and I probably are more alike than not. So, I do think we both could have been spawned from the same scene. I think where you are born and grow up decides what kind of experiences you are going to have and what kind of culture you are going to be exposed to. Yet, I also think it's more about the personality of a person that decides whether he or she is going to listen to this weird loud music.

Although your musical roots go back to Revolution Summer in D.C. and the beginnings of Soulside, you really became an entrenched musical partisan of the 1990s, an era partly documented in the new photo book Rat-a-Tat Tat. Sam McPheeters from Men's Recovery Project has characterized the 1990s as a time when "Repeat infusions of disposable cash. And spare time brought out the talent in everybody.This was a good-looking decade. Is such a large percentage of the population really so talented, or was this but a cash-induced artificial bubble of national creativity?" Do you agree with his assessment of an era "almost as inaccessible to us" as the time of President Coolidge?

I think that's a pretty lofty assessment of that time. I don't know if it was cash as much as it was the right time for a convergence of energy, novelty, and age. By the late 80s, there was a well-organized network of cities to play, and punk rock was everyone's hobby. And it just grew, so in the 90s all these people are young and ready to be starving musicians. If you went to college or post-college in D.C., and were of a certain inclination, you played music, held a crappy job, and tried to play. Then you went off to Baltimore, Richmond or Chicago, where you met your counter-part, same clothes and attitudes, just different people in different locations. I also think any time a photo book comes out, it lends credibility. A good-looking published book must make it real and important or why else would someone go through the trouble? But the pictures distort reality to an extent; you never really see how few people were in the audience and how microscopic it all was.

By the way, are those your drawings on the back of Soulsides' first album (credited to Chris)? Did you have anything to do with the sunflower iconography that stayed with the band throughout its graphic history?

I did the drawings and came up with the logo, the sun etc. It went through some mutations as different people did the artwork.

Has punk become so nostalgic and retro (whether it's recycled Gang of Four, Psychic TV, or Television, to ham on rye street punk bands) that it is really is no different than Phish deadhead revivalism? You've called it "the cyclical nature of things," which is obvious, but Psychic TV really sounded very little like anything before, so whereas they forged new territory, are we now just forging mimicry, or what you call, "Xerox copycat bands"?

I have my own conspiracy theories. But I would say it's a total deadhead revisionism scenario. But, I think it's where we are at as a culture and it plays into my idea that everyone is so busy trying to be successful that creativity and originality suffers. No one wants to take chances and fall on his or her face. That's why Psychic TV really didn't sound like anyone else, because they weren't trying. Nowadays, people want to follow a structure, a tired and true course, like, "Let's riff on this." It's because there aren't any personalities any more. And then other people want to get famous, but it's across the board with movies, art, fashion, and everything.

I just saw the Incredible Mr. Limpet when I gave the DVD to my wife for X-Mas, and you have half-jokingly said there should be a "critical reevaluation of Don Knotts including his wardrobe from Three's Company." In a way, wasn't Don Knotts a better barometer of culture than anything produced by Andy Warhol or the beats, because he was working fully within the confines and vernacular of mainstream America, thus subverting them?

Don Knotts was a talented comedic actor, but an actor none-the-less, which makes him a whore; actors will do anything to get work/ money. So, I don't think Don Knotts was living out some subversive plan. I think he dressed and acted how other people told him too. If you think about why was poor Don Knotts still working on *Three's Company* when he should have been retired (editor's note: Chris leaves the reader to contemplate the painful reality of his assertion).

You are, undeniably, a lover of pun, inversion, and irony, as the title "Let them Eat the Monorchid" suggests, let alone your spiel about the less-than-rebellious stadium rock punk of the late 1980s and their indie rock little brothers: "What we're sick of are these non-committals (i.e. indie

rockers) who watched quietly as their baby-boomer parents, unable to deal with their older siblings' mohawks, enlisted the aid of psychiatric facilities at an unprecedented level during the early-to-mid-'80s. It is often this younger generation, having been coerced by familial guilt, that thinks twice about engaging in life-threatening rebellion, so they opt for a more gentle lifestyle whose soundtrack consists of the amateurish yet palatable organic sounds of musical groups associated with the Pacific Northwest." Is this sardonic nature just your bored reaction to music writers, press coverage, and semesters, or is it just a tried and true part of your personality?

I try not to be so angry and bitter anymore. I was just giving the finger to this whole notion of indie rock; it just always seems so homogenized and tepid. Punk rock lite. I always wondered where the confrontation went. Maybe it was because I was young, but I remember going to these shows that were very life or death. You traveled to these shitty, sketchy neighborhoods, you saw bands like Black Flag on the "My War" tour, and it was just a big fist fight and there would be people on acid and drunk and the weirdo art people there too. Maybe, now, I think it's all silly, but that's really what I got off on was this whole feeling you never knew what was going to happen next. You got punched, the singer threw the mic stand in the audience, and then it seemed overnight things got so damn neighborly. And you sit there with a shit-eating smile listening to crappy music munching on vegan brownies as some girl does a spoken word piece about her sexual abusive family.

"I'm a big fan of Bob Schick of Honor Role fame, Daniel Higgs is inspiring, most of the punk stuff I have been into has had real snotty vocals, like Keith Morris, Tony Cadena, Bobby Pyn," you told one interviewer. What do you think of Daniel's new Jew's harp album, and what do you think of someone like Keith Morris, who despite injury and disease, seems to avoid the adage "Live Fast Die Young" and still be a potent, albeit near retirement age, force in music?

I respect Keith Morris way more than I do a lot of people. At this point, it's the only thing he knows how to do. I think he's earned our respect, so let's treat him as an artist. I am certainly not a fan of Jew's harp (is it PC to call it that?), but I am a fan of Dan Higgs. I think you realize the importance of people like Dan Higgs and Keith Morris the longer they are around, so it makes sense to document their artistic vision. Check out Keith Morris on the new Wrangler Brutes recording.

To you, "The best creative ideas are most visceral full of heart so that the musician does not have to hide behind studio trickery, or overtraining." Is that why the new Red Eyed Legends record is so entirely raw sounding, unfiltered, even more so than the Dirtbombs, or on par with Guitar Wolf? Is a return to the ideas of Smithsonian Folkways Archive, simply a document of a live experience, or is it reverse studio trickery?

I've been trying to capture the live experience for years. I'm not a snob and I love overproduced, beautiful sounding records. Sadly, the authentic Red Eyed Legends sound has never seen the light of day. The promo CDs that got sent out were a rough mix version and un-mastered, so chances are the CD you possess is the wrong shitty sounding version, but thanks for your generous compliment. We've since added a permanent keyboard and are recording for an LP and spilt single.

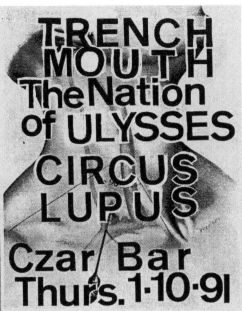

TRENCH
MOUTH
The Nation
of ULYSSES
CIRCUS
LUPUS
Czar Bar
Thurs. 1·10·91

VIRUS
P.ZA BONOMELLI, 3 (ZONA P. CORVETTO)
Concerto CON:
IGNITION
(WASHINGTON D.C.)
SO MUCH HATE
(NORVEGIA)
SABATO 7 NOVEMBRE
INIZIO: ORE 21

IGNITION
LAUGHING
HYENAS
JULY 29
DC SPACE

the monorchid
broken hearts are blue
endeavor
closer

july

all-ages, $5 7pm-bish bish

By Janet Morgan

An interview with J. Robbins

Originally printed in Left of the Dial 2002.

Steadfast should be J. Robbins middle name. As throbbing bass player for Washington D.C's godfathers of punk Government Issue during the late-1980s, or as angular, jazz-inflected guitarist and clean-voiced, freewheeling singer poet for post-punks Jawbox, and now as the same captain of cool for Burning Airlines, Robbins has always put integrity above profit while making albums that sound wide-open one minute, and restrained the next.

Whereas late era Government Issue yanked a few elements from the Damned and, along with Scream, put rock'n'roll back into the D.C. soundscape, Jawbox shifted gears towards more abstract and stylized sound structures that left listeners both enthralled and vexed. Between their well-honed, seminal albums "For Your Own Special Heart" (Atlantic, 1994) and "Jawbox" (Atlantic, 1996), Robbins charged ahead by writing lyrics felt like Bob Dylan's leftover notes from *Tarantula*, and played with popular punk tastes by delving into covers of Joy Division, Big Boys, and the Avengers.

Burling Airline continues the same trajectory, but flirts with early, oddball XTC and big guitar music while not giving up their trademark funky and ferocious drumming. There's even acoustic touches, and yikes, balladry. Lumped in with Shellac as post-punk saviors, Burning Airlines proves that music is still a wishing well, and their live shows prove that Robbins is always ready for the metaphoric kill.

You once said that not making music would be a bad thing for you. Explain.

I kind of feel that it's a self-explanatory kind of remark. Because I can't imagine a life without it, though sometimes not going on the road and eating breakfast at Denny's every morning and sleeping on the floor seems like a good idea. But making music seems essential.

You could never walk away and just produce bands?

Even if we broke up this band tomorrow and I decided I was going to work in the studio for the rest of my life, you know I love working in the studio, I would still want to be making music somehow. It's just essential. At the point when my old band Jawbox broke up, I tried to be a graphic designer for about a year. I had little ideas for songs, but I was so bummed that I didn't have a band. I had no place to take these songs to, no one to work them out with, and I was working all the time at my job. At first, I was like, this was the new era of my life where I will get fulfillment from this other kind of work. And I really started to hate it very quickly. And the minute we started playing together in this band everything just got better. It was just like, yes! All this music stuff that was getting backed up in my head had an outlet, and it just felt really good, so I kind of took that as a lesson.

Supposedly, Burning Airlines' *Mission: Control!* was a record you had wanted to make for a long time. Why?

It's funny because I don't necessarily feel that's true. My approach to doing music is much more in the moment than doing that. Rather than envisioning a goal and then trying to achieve it, it's like sitting down and seeing what comes out at and seeing where it leads you. Next thing, you have parts of a song, and put it together with everybody, and you keep doing that until you have a bunch and see what works on a record. It's more process-driven and not so much like, well, we've done two records of three minute pop songs so now it's time to conquer the rock opera.

Time for *Tommy!*

Exactly. So what was cool about starting this band and doing the first record was that it was the record I had been waiting to make for a long time in the sense that it was the first record I made from a position of confidence, as opposed to total self-doubt. Like I was pretty sure when we were making that record that we had a good idea of how things should sound and we were going to execute it well. I didn't know necessarily that it was going to be a good record, but I knew that we could do what we set out to do and we were going to have fun doing it and it would be the best record we could make. At the end of it all, we were really happy with it, which is why we started coming out and touring. So this record is the first record this band has made as a band.

As a cohesive unit.

Yeah, here we are, we've gone out on tour a bunch. I mean, Bill and I were tight to a certain extent because we toured together in Jawbox so much.

But with Jawbox, I've heard that it was almost like hand-to-hand combat with everybody putting his or her hands on a song and shaping it. Even a song that you might bring in almost done ended up morphing quite a bit, which I imagine was frustrating.

But it's also one of the beautiful things about having a band. I never enjoyed the idea of being a dictator. I mean, there's some songs in this band that I can point to and say, I am the songwriter of that song. That is my song, but only in the sense that it emerged from the group process without being radically altered from what I initially heard in my head. I think that we are all more comfortable with the idea that someone comes in, and the person is usually me, with a vision, or broad idea of where the song goes. And then it's a much more finished skeleton that gets built into the whole arrangement, whereas with Jawbox it was like start jamming and get a headache and then hear when somebody else came across something you liked then you waved your arms and went, wait, wait, wait! What was that you just did? Do that again, do that again, and they'd be like, what are talking about? It was everybody negotiating like that. It wasn't really like combative, but it was cacophonous and four egos secretly or publicly to some degree saying, it's my song.

So it's just about another form of songwriting? For instance, you've talked about making your song lyrics more accessible.

A little bit, but I also have to, because I'm the only lyric writer in this band, where in Jawbox everything was collaborative. Some songs are more mine, and some songs pretty much everybody had their hand in. There's some songs in Jawbox where you really couldn't say whose it was, but it wouldn't have been a song if Zach hadn't written an amazing beat, and had strong sense of what should go around it. Or at least a strong sense of what he didn't like. And everyone pitched in licks.

The Jawbox lyrics seem like free association and sometimes barely hang together.

I think it's fairly still true with this band, though it's been a conscious effort to try and streamline the lyrics and make more coherent and immediate lyrics. But it's difficult for me to do because I am really addicted to a certain process, which is more like throwing out more interesting and cool, well whose to say they are interesting and cool, I mean just putting together things that feel good to sing that are suggestive or something and jamming up a couple of those next to each other and see what kind of meaning they can create and where that leads. Kind of like free association almost in therapy. Like, what am I really trying to say when I have all this stuff.

That style is also epitomized by Jets to Brazil, and for a long time by Michael Stipe from R.E.M.

The other thing is that I want to get them down to a fine point, but it's very difficult, because as a listener I really love lyrics that are rich in interpretations, ones that can be interpreted in many different ways. Like one of the things I get off on in life is contextualizing things in different ways, like digging up meaning in commonplace stuff, or different ideas about stuff you randomly write. Having fun with the way that meanings can spin off of things is really a great sort of pleasure for me creatively and in life, but when it comes to lyrics I sometimes let myself get astray in order to see where I am actually going. So I think the thing I want to do is to try and make sure that, I sound like such a hippie it's ridiculous.

Or like a beatnik?

If I'm going to do that process, I want to make sure that the point I'm led to is really clear to the person who is going to hear the song, because the more I do music and the more that I listen to songs, the ones that really stick to me are really direct.

Would that include Cole Porter?

Yeah, and those are songs that are really rich in imagery. You have no doubt. Like "Lush Life" is a strangely meandering, strangely constructed song with a lot of goofy internal rhymes, but what it is about is unquestionable. You totally feel it.

So the point is to reach a balance and create an interesting tension between lyrics and instrumentation.

That's the genius of Billy Strayhorn, who can write a lyric like "Lush Life", or Andy Partridge from XTC can write lyrics that can get off on their own internal rhymes and word play, but they have a really soulful, honest core that is communicating something of value and revealing something of the songwriter. That's an amazing gift to me, and I can't imagine even having it.

When I think about the covers done by Jawbox and Burning Airlines, like the Avengers, Minutemen, Cure, Big Boys, Echo and Bunnymen and others, the music may morph considerably, but there's always a strong emphasis on the intensity of the lyrics.

That's really cool, thank you for listening so closely. It's actually really true. And this is something I've never talked to anybody about, even in the band. When I choose a cover, it's because the lyrics really speak to me and I feel like I can sing it with real conviction. Otherwise, it's like okay, let's have fun with the music. Though I think that Bunnymen cover is actually verbatim, there's just no brass.

The Avengers "Thin White Line" and Big Boys "Sound on Sound" are considerably morphed. But then you have the traditional version of the Buzzcocks' "Airwaves Dream."

To tell you the truth, the Buzzcocks' cover is a bit embarrassing because we couldn't have done the Buzzcocks as good as they did themselves. And with the Big Boys, we couldn't have done a better arrangement than them. And with the Avengers, not only could you have not done it as good as them, but also Jawbox was never a band that was any good at playing a three chord punk song. It's music we really love, but we felt really stupid doing it. Beyond a certain point Well, I know Bill felt this way, and I always felt this way, when I go to reach for a bar chord, when I'm just playing the chord, it's so satisfying. But if I try and make a song out of it, it's just impossible, and I just feel like I am cheating, like someone gave me a handicap. It takes a really special circumstance to be excused.

But though you have talked about streamlining the lyrics, and perhaps simplifying things a bit, on the new record you write on one song, "You can't trust a simple song."

That's a lyric you can look at from two sides. That was a bit of an accusation to me. That's me kind of accusing myself of being a cheap songwriter and just getting revenge. That's the raison d' etre for whatever I did for many years, like getting revenge in a song. And that's a little bit of cheating. And that's not the worst thing you can do as a songwriter, but if that's the only thing you do that's pretty sad. So that song, "Lexicon", is a little bit of me chastising myself and say c'mon, rise above, you can do better than just write a song that doesn't just say, fuck you to stuff that pisses you off, couched in special secret terms. So that's one thing about it. I'm chastising myself and pointing a finger at myself because I can't trust a simple song.

You can't trust that three-chord formula.

A lot of people have written great songs that way, but for me I feel lazy. And in some ways it's true, it's totally easy to be distrustful of a simple song, because if you just let shit happen, you get Blink 182, and that's not a good thing.

Another lyrics is, "Don't say it again, try something new," which seems to echo the poet William Carlos Williams when he said, "Make it new" decades ago. But at what point does trying to make it new become used up or redundant?

I don't think so, just because I think that for me, at least in my experience, it's impossible to write with any other process. It's more about, what do I want to write about, like let's find some different things to write about.

So it's not about structure, but subject?

It's not about the structure of the song. Even if someone hears our band and thinks it's complicated, strange, art rock monstrosity, I guess I can see that. But to me it's simple, completely normal rock music. And when you break down our songs, they go verse chorus, verse chorus, bridge, chorus for the most part. I think that's a structure that has a lot of life left in it, because to me it's more about trying to find interesting ways for the four people in the band to get their ideas together and listen to each other. Like if a bass line leads in a certain way, it's about me trying to follow through with that process by coming up with a melody that works with it in a way that's satisfying and unexpected.

So again, what about subject matter?

Well, see, that's a new thing to me, because before I didn't feel that I had that much control over what I was going to write about. It was always just stuff that was eating at me that I couldn't deal with rationally, so I would make a little voodoo doll in the form of a song. Now, I really want to go beyond doing that. I'm really in awe of people that can choose a topic and write a song about it, like Phil Ochs, or Bob Dylan.

Like pointing to a headline in the paper and saying, "That is it."

But Phil Och's best songs, to me, are his personal ones, like "Crucifixion." It's a crazy song because it has these crazy rambling lyrics that feel like he is really upset. It doesn't really cohere, but you really know what it's about.

It might last longer than "Cops of the World" simply because of its intimacy.

But "Cops of the World" works in the world today! But with "Crucifixion," when you hear it, it really grips you, you know it's the result of seeing the death of J.F.K., but it's also about the loss of innocence. It's a fucking monster of a song. It's so amazing.

The new record has the song "Morricone Dancehall", while the last album had a clip from Orson Welles' *The Trial*. Did these have anything to do with your love of soundtrack music as a kid?

No, it's not a conscious one, because "Morricone Dancehall" happened because Mike had that bass line, which I was totally in love with, and both of us kind of had an infatuation with dancehall music, so we cooked up the dancehall beat on the drum machine, then I started jamming to his bass line, and I came up with.

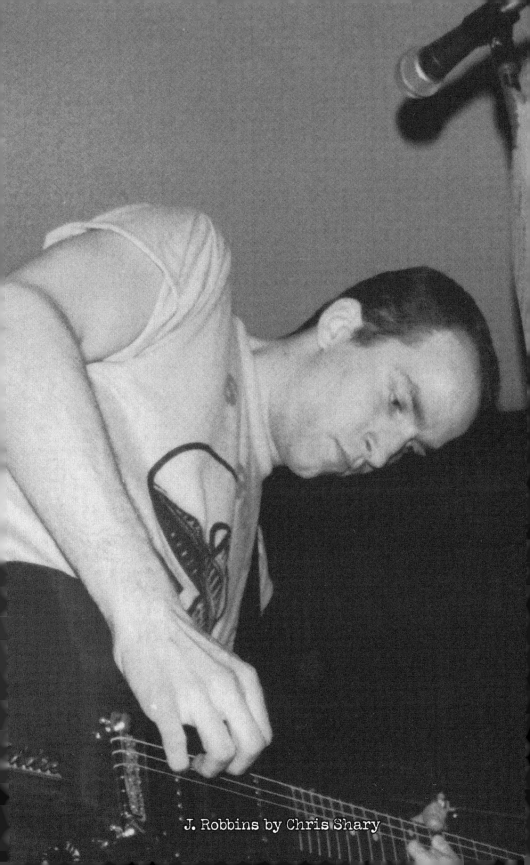

J. Robbins by Chris Shary

When you say dancehall, do you mean R&B music?

Well, Jamaican dancehall music like Yellowman. Dancehall is pretty sick music. It's so minimal and stripped down, with nothing but voice and a rhythm, and it's so aggressive. It's not even like hip hop beats that can be kind of laid back. So anyway, I had this guitar line that I thought sounded like a spaghetti western, so it was just a working title that stuck.

I know you loved Beethoven's 7th Symphony, so how does listening to that and Tangerine Dream at an early age shape your idea of creating a whole soundscape with each song?

Well, I don't really know, but I know that because I listened to a lot of film music when I was younger, it kind of fucked up my ideas of song structures. Maybe that's why now I love verse chorus verse chorus etc., because film music, in a way, is the worst music to listen to because it has no structure at all, because it's structured around the visuals.

That's why I suppose it is called incidental music.

It really responds and heightens. The form of film music is dictated by whatever the action it is trying to heighten, so it's not symphonic form or song form, but a lot of film music has a strong sense of melody. It's either really strong in melody, or really strong in texture, and a lot of the music I was into was really strong on mood and texture. It was all the music you didn't remember hearing later, but made the murder scene more scary, or the love scene more passionate. So maybe it makes me Well, lately it makes me think about, though I don't know if it's exactly right but I presume, that it's influence makes me think more about texture. I love playing the electric guitar, but I don't feel like much of a guitarist. I feel like it's just a matter of convenience because it's the most familiar instrument, so when I go to do a song, it's the most immediate way of hashing through it and getting parts on the table. Lately, I'm much more interested in making a guitar not sound like a guitar. I'm hoping that it's going to be less of a rocky rock band.

Not unlike Joe Strummer being very influenced by *Apocalypse Now* and making records that have Third World texture and grooves, like the second half of *Combat Rock*, when he seems to have an almost cinematic approach.

You know, I never got that impression. I just thought it was a big melting pot of influences, like listening to old Motown records.

But like you are listening to dancehall music, the Clash were listening to reggae and early hip-hop.

That's one of the things that makes the Clash such a great band. Now, there are bands like Dismemberment Plan that I think do that brilliantly. I think they're the best melting pot.

Mixing different types of media?

Like they love so much contemporary R&B and hip-hop and they steal from it in ways that that never seem that they are doing a bullshit thing like, this is a rock band doing a hip-hop groove. They just incorporate it. They just feed on it, and the things that come out are Dismemberment Plan songs. But I don't know if my interest in films really bears that much relation to our vision of our band.

You once said that "I don't know what mainstream is," but that Britney Spears is Pat Boone-ish, though with a layer of pornography on top.

It's giving people what they want. It's the pretense of innocence.

You've also said that people are speaking the same language. Does that mean it has been corporatized?

It's hard to make a simple analysis like that, like to say that whatever was underground has been bought up by the corporate culture machine. Yet, you can say that because it's definitely true.

We are seeing Violent Femmes and Iggy Pop songs used as advertising on nighttime TV.

Well, homogeneity happens.

So what should make punk any different?

Yeah. I think it's much more interesting and scary, and unfathomable and compelling to me, the way that the language, pace, and attitude of advertising has taken over human interaction in way that I feel that a lot of times that instead of people talking to each other they are pitching to each other. The way we collectively discuss our existence in the West is mostly through television. The way we know about each other is from watching TV, so somebody in Kansas knows about N.Y.C. because they watch TV. That's a stupid simplification, but the language, the editing and sound, the visual media is so complicated, and there's many layers of meaning that are in it that aren't even intended in advertising. And people don't even think about the extra layers of meaning necessarily in what they're creating, they just think about pitching the product. But they pitch it in this incredible evolved, hyper language that people just receive. So, I think there is a lot of the information that we can't process directly, and I think it's reasonable to sort of speculate that we act on it, and it changes the way that we behave.

J.G. Ballard pursued such ideas a lot in the 1970s, suggesting that we are being shaped by forces that we are mostly unaware of, like how the lingo used at the office and newspeak shapes our identity.

You know that I love J.G. Ballard. It makes sense to me. It's a language that millions, if not billions, of people are trapped in the flow of. A language that has meanings that can't all be really accounted for, like whether Tommy Hilfiger logos mean something beyond the fact that he makes clothes. Because it all means something about status in a certain community, and the fact that it was made by sweatshop laborers half way around the world. There are stacks and stacks of meanings.

All interconnected.

How are people not shaped by language, because how else do we communicate?

Well, our language is mediated by forces that we don't necessarily control, so even people who are deep into hip-hop or punk don't understand that they are mechanisms of a larger force.

And that's what is so bizarre to me. I don't blame anybody for tuning out completely, because there is no way in which you are not a target market. It's such a true statement to me, that I don't really blame anybody for tuning out of the whole idea, for just not wanting to address it. I just read a book about monochondrial DNA as way of tracing maternal genealogy. It was written by this guy who does genetic research at Oxford and he was able to basically. Well he did all this research and came up with the assertion that almost everybody of Western European descent can ultimately trace their maternal genealogy to seven different women who lived in the beginning and end of the first ice age. It's an amazing book. But he just drops this bomb at the end of the book, just mentions it in passing, that he was at a conference with these chemical companies who are talking about patenting DNA, because it's just a chemical like any other. And if they did the research, and discovered a certain strand of DNA, then its intellectual property.

So we can all be owned by somebody!

And you and I can talk about how insane that is, and so many people that I know will agree that it's completely insane. Of course it's insane, you don't even have to think about it. But then there's someone else who's got shit loads of money, corporate sponsorship and a legal team who is just looking at the profit motive, and are going yeah, we can totally own that DNA. That's so insane! But they are like, why shouldn't we? You are interfering with our rights by preventing us from patenting this DNA. It's completely out of control.

But it seems like, at times, in Jawbox's lyrics you were opting out of that language, and creating lyrics that resembled French playwright Artaud, or French Surrealist and Dadaist poets.

That rules (laughs)! That makes me really happy, but I am also flip flopping back and forth between things all the time, and I really don't want to crawl up my own ass and be an artist that makes stuff that doesn't make sense to anybody just to be capricious. There are times that I am literally dying about my inability to write a straightforward song. That's what I am dying to hear. Because when I hear a simple song, now here's an example of advertising, when I hear a simple song that I can trust, I want to cling to it and kiss it, and say thank you, thank you, never leave me. It's like a tonic, knowing that someone has a simple desire to communicate, especially about the insanity of this world, of the circumstances we are in. I think it's really precious and really amazing. That's why in my mind there's times when I sit down to write lyrics and I am almost desperate to say something simple, and then I despair because I just can't because I feel like am cheating. But that's psychobabble. I'm letting it all hang out! The alternative is that it feels like running advertising copy to write a simple song.

Like unlike rock writing. When I write a preview, I'm the PR person creating a spiel.

We just toured with Shiner in the Midwest, I think they are so awesome. The things that people wrote about them was so funny, because they kept get tagged as heavy emo.

(both laugh)

But I thought about it, like what would I say? Come to the fucking show. Because that's all I feel comfortable saying about bands that I really love. Like the Dismemberment Plan. What are they? What kind of music is that? It's great fucking music. Come to the show. Any time I can say, those guys, yeah, they're emo, it's just a dismissal. Even though there's amazing hip hop music being made, if I say hip hop, chances are I'm talking about something I don't like. If I'm talking about something I like, I'll say Public Enemy, or Kool Keith.

Somebody wrote that you were "an abrasive Neil Diamond, Tony Bennett type crooner, with Andrew Lloyd Webb melodiousness."

(both laugh).

That's so harsh. I'm really asking for it, but I don't care. We got to let Andrew Lloyd Webber off the hook for *Jesus Christ Superstar*. It's great. You can even fight me about it. It's good.

But "Cats" negates it! But is that quote the kind of trap we fall into when we don't want to describe it as emo?

I don't know. That sounds like character assassination to me!

I think he meant it in the best of ways.

You're in a trap if you want to write about music. I fully acknowledge that.

Could you see yourself as Andy Partridge, who still makes great, challenging records, but does not tour anymore?

I would love to see myself putting out the last two XTC records. I only want to tour as long as it is fun to tour, and it continues to be fun. Like I said, I really love working in the studio. It's a lot deeper satisfaction than playing a show. Shows are really fun too, but like anything, watching something mature over a period, and being a facilitator for somebody's creativity is really rewarding.

Is it just about twisting knobs, or about helping a band like Kerosene 454 make something fresh and challenging to them?

It is about twisting the knobs sometimes. That's one of the things that are great about it, it's a multi-level kind of enjoyment. There's many times I found great satisfaction by just finding the right application for a piece of gear to record a band that really had their shit together, and you don't have to say anything to them except, "did you tune?" Then there's other times when there's satisfaction of having the right idea that no one else thought of that turned out to be the right thing. That's a great ego boost, and also wonderful because it helps get the job done. I can see just doing that and making music, maybe at the point where my back gives out or something. I don't foresee it in the near future, for this year we've been touring most of the year. We went to Europe and Japan and the U.S. As amazing as it was, especially in Japan, if we have experiences like that than there's no reason to stop touring. I will sleep in someone's floor in Brazil, no problem! In general, our tours are with bands made up of people we really like that most of the time we already know, or we get to know them better and like them more, so it's like a fun scene. It's sometimes frustrating, but also a great way to get around.

But when do you know, as you said when Zach left Jawbox, that you are beating a dead horse?

I don't know. That's a terrible question. I have no idea, presumably you will know, it will occur to you. There's definitely been times when this band has been on tour this past year and a half where I felt that in terms of the fact that we're not in our twenties anymore, and we are not readily identifiable with any particular sub-genre rock music. We're certainly not a hardcore band, we're not an emo band, whatever that is, we're not alt country. We're sort of just this weird inbred mutant rock music that is kind of un-hypeable because we're not cute, and we don't have a shtick to dazzle people with. We just have these songs and our particular concept of doing something special and personal. So in that regard, we're not a bandwagon band, we just go out and play. There's been times when we've felt it would be easy to feel left behind in the underground music world, whatever that is. But then I think that, shit, we're in Japan. We're playing our songs there and playing with a Japanese band who we love and are our friends because we toured Japan before. Everybody knew our songs, and it was a blast. Those kinds of things have to happen, but ultimately it has to be satisfying in and of itself just to get up and play. At the point at which it's not, at the point that it is a headache to do, I think it's the point that we've over-stayed our welcome. You can't really have anything to do with second-guessing other's opinion of what you do, because that's a terrible waste of energy. Making music is not a matter of choice, if it were a matter of choice it would just be a silly hobby.

If music, at its core, is emotional, as you've said, would taking away music be like losing your emotions?

It would just be sad because I don't think you can boil music down to one thing, but it is a really great language for saying things that you can't be expressed in words in a linear way. It's an unbeatable language for going into unspoken territory and a great tool for reflection and self-analysis too.

Jawbox By John Falls

Previously unpublished excerpts from an interview with Mark Andersen from 2015

So how would you define Positive Force?

Positive Force is a collective in the fundamental meaning of that word. Essentially what we did was vote on the things people brought to the group and suggested that we do. The beneficiaries were chosen by that way- someone coming and saying here, this is a great group doing something important, how would you feel about doing a benefit? Then we might say, yeah, this is good, then the next question was, when could this happen, and that would depend upon getting a draw of bands that were drawn to the issue themselves and had an audience that could help us to raise money and consciousness by bringing out folks. If anything, I would say our tendency was to focus on the more local, but that's not entirely true. We are not a single-issue group: we were always trying to see connections. It wasn't like we said, "We're a group about this single issue and then start organizing around it." In the beginning, it was the people around the punk scene and the youth activist scene who wanted to turn rhetoric into action. There wasn't a single issue we were focused on. There are plusses and minuses to that, but overall I think that was the best approach because they are able to cover a lot of ground and raise a lot of issues in people's minds. They might be touched by one issue or another and get engaged in volunteer work. That was what we were always aiming for; that's what we were always aiming for - to get people to be activists.

Do you trace back to Revolution Summer, or particular bands, or a movement within punk?

I think it's historically true that there were two bands in particular that inspired as a group more than other. One was Crass because Crass was very much about getting up and making things happen. They were a band. Positive Force began to exist right at the end of the era when Crass existed as a band. One of their slogans at the end was, "It's not time to be fucking nice, it's time to act!" We knew they were involved with the Stop the City demonstrations, the creative, disruptive blockages that were intended to disrupt the financial district of London. It was very clear that while you might think that certain bands, even if they were interested in the right things, were more interested doing something more than just talking. Certainly that was the sense with Crass and everything they did. It was essential to act. Words were worse than nothing, basically, because they disillusion people. You talk big and you don't do anything, so why care at all? This meant there was a kind of anarchist tinge to Positive Force throughout its history. I think it's important to note PF, by and large, has resisted being affiliated with any specific left-wing tendency or group, whether socialist, communist, or small "D" democrat or anarchist. We left that intentionally vague, plus another reason for the multi-issue interest was that we wanted to create space for people to find their own definition and arena to act within. It seemed to be using the punk ethos.

The other band was 7 Seconds. They were crucial because people in and around the band formed the first Positive Force out in NV that we heard about and helped catalyze only our group but more than a dozen across the country for a time. The idea was: wherever you were, whatever punk scene, there was something you should be doing. As DOA, another influential band at the time said succinctly, "Talk minus action = zero." This was all happening before Revolution Summer. Certainly you can look at Washington D.C. and see plenty of bands that inspired people, like Bad Brains and Minor Threat. When you get to Revolution Summer, probably the biggest inspiration are Rites of Spring, Scream, Beefeater, and bands like that. Some bands had disbanded, or in the case of the Bad Brains, moved to New York City, but the bands who were still around, like Embrace and others, became crucial allies of our in making this happen. You can't see what we did outside the context of the D.C. punk scene.

Bands are bands, and if they are committed, they might have activists within the band, but they are fundamentally bands. I believe that the way bands impact people politically is first and foremost by being really good bands. The art is really important: you have to move people with your art. Otherwise it's just like me standing on the street corner spouting off. Some people may come by and listen. Unless you build an audience, you are talking to yourself, so it was crucial that we worked with bands that had this impetus and cared about things, so they might donate their services. But they were also bands that had sufficient craft and vision so that people would want to listen to them. People might criticize, to some degree fairly, Crass for being more interested in the message than in the music. I think they are a fairly unique phenomenon in that regard because it was almost like the force of their will and passion made even their more rudimentary songs moving, but there was a limit to that. I think Crass opened the door for many not-so-terribly inspired bands just as Minor Threat and Bad Brains opened the door for a number of thrash bands. It had value to the people playing. I'm not trying to put that down, but it's not as full of possibility.

For example, possibly the single most important band in Positive Force history is Fugazi. I worked with literally hundreds of bands, and I've never found a band as committed to a political vision as Fugazi. I will also say they were also as committed to their art, and that was part of what made our collaboration with them so powerful because they could do things we couldn't, and vice versa. They wanted to do protest, they wanted to do free shows, and they wanted to do benefits; in fact, that's all they did for the last thirteen years of their existence in the D.C. area. We could organize the shows, we could organize the protests that go with the shows, help flush out some of the politics in a way that hopefully would be reasonably congruent with what Fugazi thought but also give people some substance to grasp on to. We offered channels for people from hearing songs or going to a powerful concert into being at demonstrations, doing volunteer work, and educating themselves about issues. I am a student of politics and music. I have been since the mid-1970s. Without seeming silly and self-aggrandizing, I do think the alliance of Fugazi and Positive Force is one of the more significant and fruitful artistic and political collaborations that I know of, certainly in punk rock but also music in general.

Could we compare it to the MC5 and the White Panther Party?

The comparison has been made, and there is some validity to it. Certainly, I, and members of Fugazi and Positive Force were inspired by the MC5 and the White Panther Party, their energy and the way they wanted to marry music with message. Obviously, our politics ended up being somewhat distinct, given that Positive Force and Fugazi would be loosely aligned with straight-edge and MC5 was anything but. What was their slogan – "Dope, guns, and fucking in the street"? So, that was associated with them, and obviously straight-edge had some critiques of that 60's idea, both on the drugs and sex level. They also tended to have an uncritical embrace of violence as a means to change things. First, I will say that I am not a principled pacifist. I don't reject violence in all its forms. I mean, there's a long discussion about where self-defense sits in there. I think Ian from Fugazi is much more a principled pacifist, though other members of the band might not be, but certainly we share a general sense that violence is an extremely limited and crude tool.

It was not something that would generally work in our favor against the awesome force of the corporate military governmental structures, the real monopoly on tanks, guns, and bombs, but also the money. Although I would hasten to add, Positive Force or Fugazi were anarchist in the sense of seeing the state as the enemy. The state was an enemy within certain circumstances, but corporate power was just as important in our mindset, so it was less of an ideologically anarchist vision, but we did understand it as a corrective to the authoritarian left, like the Revolutionary Communist Party, which was quite active, but that group was widely rejected by the punk scene at least in D.C. because people felt they were trying to exploit our politics, our scene, for their ends and their revolution, and they didn't consult with us about what the revolution should look like.

There were remnants of the Yippies around, the 1960's radicals, the ones Jerry Rubin and Abbie Hoffman were a part of, and we mostly saw them as people that wanted to get stoned, whether it was Rock Against Reagan, Rock Against Racism, or Rock for the Legalization of Pot. It seemed to feel like it was outside of our scene. These were groups that did collaborate and did have a presence in the punk scene. Bad Brains worked closely with the Yippie folks in New York City and Washington D.C. That was kind of an exception to the rules. Although I should say, for me personally, it goes back to the MC5. I could recite word for word the opening rap from "Kick Out the Jams," or I mean "Ramblin' Rose," so they were certainly a big inspiration, as were Jefferson Airplane, Jimi Hendrix, and the Doors. But we were trying to do our own thing, and honestly I was more touched by examples of the original Rock Against Racism in England, which to a certain extent was married to the Socialist Worker's Party there.

Putting the Soul in Punk
An Interview with Soulside's Bobby Sullivan

Originally published by Razorcake's website, 2015

In a time when punk was poised to become a mere shell of its own making, no more than a hollow template for wanna-be hardcore heroes, Soulside challenged the whole pretense. Soulside tripped the body electric on punk-funk hybrids tucked into sizzling, experimental excursions. At the helm, impassioned Bobby Sullivan sang like Bob Marley rewired for the post-hardcore generation.

For thirty years, Bobby Sullivan has remained an ardent underground messenger of punk conscience. Inspired partly by the progressive playbook of Dischord Records and action-oriented community group Positive Force, whose street demonstrations swept through the nation's capital from the mid-'80s onward, Sullivan became a leading light of underground music.

Now reunited for a series of shows, including Los Angeles and San Francisco, Soulside defied simple genre categories by combining insurgent punk restlessness with neo-Third World rhythms. Sullivan helped steer the lyrical themes towards global social justice, the abolition of hate and racism, and the quest for dignity and self-determination. As his bandmates mutated into Girls Against Boys, Sullivan co-helmed Rain Like The Sound Of Trains, whose sinewy style, jolting syncopation, and humanistic themes were equally mesmerizing.

Sullivan has continued his basic idealism ever since. Based in Asheville, N.C., for years, he has advocated for prison reform, remains a firm believer in natural foods, and is a longtime promoter of sustainable farm-to-market practices, including the importance of co-ops.

If I recall, you said you are drawn to spiritual people. Does that stem from your early involvement—by way of Lunch Meat—in D.C. punk, including figures like HR of Bad Brains and Tomas of Beefeater, from other music sources, or from a sense of your own spiritual quest?

A bit of both. I was a very introspective kid and was definitely looking for direction in life outside my family life, even from an early age. A big part of it was carrying around a feeling of not fitting in, which I think a lot of people from that scene can identify with. I tried at one time to be part of what I perceived as the "popular crowd," but it just wasn't me. The complex part was that the D.C. punk scene was what my older brother Mark of Slinkees, Kingface was into, so it wasn't an automatic fit. Also, I had gotten into reggae as an alternative form of music and a link to culture, rather than punk. The turning point for me was when I realized I liked The Clash's version of "Police and Thieves" better than the original by Junior Murvin.

That's why people like HR and Tomas were so influential to me—Ian MacKaye too, in a big way—when I finally started going to shows. I found that I was not alone in appreciating various forms of non-mainstream music and more importantly, looking for ways to have a positive impact on the world. The sense of mission these big brothers had was so inspiring. These guys walked their talk, and that's how I still want to be. Faith is nothing without works, and life is about keeping on moving. To stick with what's just placed in front of you is a cop-out. I am inspired by innovators and risk takers, especially when they are rooted in something bigger than themselves. I saw the punk scene as

Bobby in Tulsa, OK, in 2015, By David Ensminger

something that could change the world, and in a lot of ways, I think it did.

Spirituality was never a thing for me that was about withdrawing from society or just how one acts on Sundays. It's about how interconnected we all are, no matter how different we perceive ourselves to be. And our actions are like pebbles thrown into a pond. As small as the splash may be, their effect ripples out in expanding circles, which eventually reach the shore. I've always felt that there is a responsibility to do good, which goes along with being an artist, especially if you are broadcasting your art from a massive sound system or distributing it around the world in the form of commodities. Of course, we all may differ on what "good" is, but that's part of the fun!

On stage in Tulsa, Okla., in September you sang with Scream. What appeals to you most about their legacy—is it a personal connection, their sense of blurring and fusing genres, or their commitment to a sense of punk conscience?

Scream is a band that has always had melody and heart. I was never into music that has monotonous screaming. Intensity? Yes, but it has to have melody. Like the Bad Brains, Scream typified what Bob Marley sang about in "Punky Reggae Party" and what happened when The Clash played with Steel Pulse at the Rock Against Racism shows in England. Punk and reggae grew up together, which was how it was for me. It's strange now to see the disconnect between the two genres. Even fans of both seem to have no idea of the connection. It wasn't lost on Poland, though. When we went there in 1989, their punk scene had just as many reggae bands as punk bands, even though they were behind the Iron Curtain.

I think it was fitting that I got to sing a Jacob Miller cover with Scream in Tulsa because like Scream, the Bad Brains, and The Clash, most of the punk bands I ended up loving had at least one reggae song in their set—as did Lunch Meat, the first incarnation of Soul Side. I'm talking about bands like DOA, Operation Ivy, and British bands like the Ruts, the Slits, Stiff Little Fingers, and Generation X, who had a dub version of one of their songs. Don Letts in the British scene was someone who really got it. He ended up in Big Audio Dynamite with Mick Jones from The Clash, but earlier on he had filmed one of Bob Marley's videos and had been the DJ that played reggae songs in between sets at punk shows in London.

I believe you mentioned that, in some ways, Rage Against The Machine seemed to embody what you envisioned Soul Side might have been. I always felt as if Rains Like The Sound Of Trains came close to that heavy, syncopated riffage, like the 1993 single "Bad Man's Grave."

It's a bit of an oversimplification, but in the way that we were blending genres and broadcasting ideas, I think Rage Against The Machine blew the roof off of it. In the mid-'80s, punk music was evolving from the earlier template forged by Black Flag and Minor Threat, among many others. A conversation that really typifies this happened at a show in Ann Arbor, where we were opening up for DOA. After our set, I went back to the T-shirt booth and continued hanging out with the singer from the Beatnigs, the opening band—yes, it was Michael Franti Beatnigs, The Disposable Heroes of Hiphoprisy. He said, "You guys remind me of a band from the West Coast called Jane's Addiction." It was the first time I had heard of them, and I'm pretty sure they didn't have anything out yet. It wasn't that we sounded so much alike, but rather that the blend of grooves with the intensity of punk was a new thing. I think Rage did it better than anyone.

You manage a co-op in Asheville and have been a long-time supporter of

the movement. Did this, by chance, originate from your experience with Dischord or Positive Force—the concept that people can voluntarily organize businesses and outreach groups with an alternative game plan?

Working for co-ops is very much a continuation of what I felt like I was participating in with the punk scene. It's a right livelihood, just like being in the kind of band we were in. The way co-ops support the communities they are in is fundamentally different than what a Whole Foods does. The corporate stores just pretend to be community-oriented, which is just like the difference between Dischord and a major label. In fact, the way Dischord is run is a major influence for how I run the co-op I now manage.

It just so happened that the first co-op I worked for was near Dischord House and Positive Force House. Ian MacKaye was a big supporter and regular shopper, as were many folks from Positive Force. In fact, most of the co-op's staff members were part of Positive Force, as well as our chapter of Food Not Bombs. So, there was a real continuity there. Even today, the co-op I manage works hard to have authentic relationships with the owners, shoppers, and local activists who are involved in issues around food.

In my mind, there are many similarities between co-ops and the punk scene we were part of because both settings empower leadership, education, and freedom of expression. They also incubate local businesses and encourage working with others toward a common end, which, like Dischord, has a really profound effect on the community they serve. And both encourage innovation instead of just copying what has come before, or what's in the mainstream. It's my solid belief that co-ops are the answer for the world's economic and social woes. Small local companies are cool, but too often sell out once they get a chance. Co-ops are structurally so different, that if a decision is made to sell out, it is because a majority of stake holders have decided that is the best way to go, rather than just a single entrepreneur. Those stake holders—workers, community members, et cetera—all benefit as well, instead of just that one person who started the business.

For me, your more recent songs like "70's Heroes," though lush, layered, and acoustic, seem to expand where songs from *Trigger* left off - especially the re-imagining of "War"—or tunes from Rain Like The Sound Of Trains, including "Branching Out." How have you sustained a faith in that sense of social justice, underground revolutionary spirit, and music as a way to narrate neglected history?

I just can't leave the approach behind. I'm possessed with getting crucial information out there. It used to be that alternative histories were just suppressed. Today, with the internet, there is so much misinformation going on, it's going to take people who have an actual connection to the facts to speak their truths. And unfortunately, the loudest voices are generally the most extreme ones, so the authentic stories get drowned out. They need to be shared as much as possible, and we really need to rekindle our personal connections, for this modern age makes everyone feel more connected while they really become more isolated.

Take, for instance, Rastafari. That was a movement that if you wanted to know about it, you really had to talk to someone. You had to find an elder, if possible, and reach outside of your immediate comfort zone to sit, reason, and receive. You could also find a small bookstore where you would likely be called out for your interests and challenged on what you might know and what more you're looking to find out. It was and is a culture of exchange between people who are face-to-face. I used to seek this kind of interaction out in every city I went to, and there were some great spots and great people to learn from in D.C. It wasn't always easy, but it was authentic and challenging, in a good way.

Today, you can just go online and get all kinds of weird shit coming at you while you just sit, isolated at your computer—homophobia, patriarchal nonsense, insane biblical fallacies, race-based extremism, et cetera. Sure, some of that would come out in the past, but the experience I had with it was more inclusive and personal. People couldn't just hurl insults around and then block you to keep you from responding. We are truly social beings that thrive on a give and take, so our history and culture is really related to others within our proximity, which is more honest when it is shared. Ideas are powerful and yet very dangerous when we harbor ones that haven't been vetted by a community of real people, rather by internet personas.

In fact I have a book, which will hopefully be coming out, that takes the subject matter of my songs to a new level. Each chapter is based on a song and provides the background information I used to write the song. My intention is to provide a trail of authors and sources that are mostly hard to find, or at least not as common as what we all have in our faces. This way, if the subject matter is intriguing, further research can be done by the reader. It's like a lyric sheet on steroids.

Hot Bodi-Gram seemed to move towards more abstract, emotive, and purely poetic lyrics ("Punch the geek / ego speaks"), almost foreshadowing the direction of other bands like Jawbox. Was the songwriting process different? What inspired those pieces—the catacombs in Paris, visions of a deceased friend, a soured D.C. scene?

We wrote that album while on tour, so it was very collaborative, and we were able to get audience feedback, rather than just going to a studio and recording a bunch of new songs. The tour was six months long—two months in the U.S. and four in Europe—so we worked on the music at sound checks and introduced new songs as they got close enough to being finished, which helped us refine them night after night. We took all that energy from the tour right into the studio with us, as the final show was basically our recording session in a studio outside of Amsterdam. Henry Rollins's European sound guy was the engineer, and Eli, our sound guy who had been on the whole tour, was the producer. This was our first time not having Ian MacKaye as the producer. Previously, he had produced everything we recorded.

Part of the reason the lyrics were a bit different than before was because the band was just evolving. I was interested in crafting messages in a more poetic way and some members of the band were sick of doing interviews about our political and/or social beliefs, so it was a good opportunity to try something a little different. I'm all about the message, but it's my feeling that sometimes you can have a greater effect when you are not so blatant about what you are trying to say, which I think can give the messages a bit more traction. Realization comes later, rather than just when you first hear the song. Messages can eke out in a progressive way.

You helped start the D.C. chapter of the Anarchist Black Cross, helped stir the Foods Not Bombs chapter, and have worked with prisoners as part of a Rastafarian outreach program in North and South Carolina (Rastafarian UniverSoul Order Prison Ministry). Musicians from Johnny Cash to Jail Guitar Doors have also reached out to inmates. What makes this work so fulfilling? Even when you worked at RAS Records, you were sending home-taped music to inmates, correct?

FROM ORANGE COUNTY, CALIFORNIA

Last Rites
PRESENTS

AGENT ORANGE

SCREAM

FROM NEW YORK CITY
UNDER-DOG

SOULSIDE

I'M GOIN, YOU? / M= TOO! / PHUK! YEAH! / GMPH. / YUP!

-Bob

SUNDAY,
JULY 31ST
Tickets at the door

CUBBY BEAR
1059 WEST ADDISON · 327.1662
ALL AGES

Doors Open 6:00
Show Starts 6:30

FLIPSIDE's — Best New Band of 1987

SOULSIDE

DISCHORD
DISCHORD
DISCHORD

From Wash D.C.
FRI AUG 19th
w/ Special Guests

9 PM
THe GRove
1618 E. 17 DEN.
18 ID REZ
$5. DOOR

WESTERN WASTE

$4 Adv
at WAX TRAX (DtW)
Albums on the Hill (Boulr)

Tix available

MOVE IT ● HYPE
NEW L.P. OUT NOW DISCHORD

IT'S YOUR UNDERGROUND

FROM WASHINGTON D.C.

DISCHORD

RECORDING ARTISTS

SOULSIDE
WITH
A PRIORI
AMERICAN STANDARD
PHALLIC ATROCITIES

$5 $5

ALL AGES(21 AND OVER CAN DRINK)
CALL DAN 201-993-5985 FOR FURTHER INFO.

SUN. JUNE 12, 8 PM SHESKEZ
155 Howe Ave PASSAIC NJ 201-777-9211

WED.
July
27th

$5.00!

Starts at
8:00
-Sharp

SOULSIDE

Break your
FACE

Hey Jr INFO:

AMERICAN STANDARD

Chris

Working at RAS Records was where I got my first introduction to some of the challenges inmates in the U.S. experience. Johnny (the bass player of Soulside) and I both worked there and we did the mail order, which meant we were responding to tons of letters from people ordering reggae albums—this included inmates. Johnny and I engaged in extended correspondence with many of them, and as we learned about their financial challenges, we actively taped albums from our own collections to send them so they wouldn't have to pay for every album they were interested in.

Later, the work I did in the Anarchist Black Cross put me in touch with revolutionaries from the '60s and '70s who were behind bars, and some who had gotten out. This was different because these were political prisoners and prisoners of conscience, not folks incarcerated for crimes—although many times there isn't much of a difference between to the two. Marilyn Buck was one person who I corresponded with for years. I ended up putting one of her poems to music, and she critiqued an early version of my book. The dialogue I had with her over that period of time was priceless, and it was bittersweet to see her get out of prison just to die two weeks later of cancer. She had only been released so she could die with her relatives. I highly recommend looking into her story, as she was a white person who effectively worked with the Black Liberation Movement.

All this led to my work with the RUO. When Ras Marley moved to where I live in North Carolina, I was highly motivated to get involved. Ras Marley is an ordained minister, so he is able to represent Rastafari in an official capacity according to the prison guidelines. Rastafari is a recognized religion within the U.S. prison system, so Rastas have the same rights of worship as any other recognized religion. Members of the RUO, including myself, are able to visit prisons ranging from minimum to maximum security in the South, conducting "religious services" for the brethren. That means we can bring in drums and have a whole day with them, chanting, reasoning, and showing videos.

The prisoners have told us that our "services" are the only ones that draw people from multiple religions. At our events, we have Jewish, Nation of Islam, Muslim, Moorish Science, Christian, Native American brothers, and more. Many are inspired by the example of Haile Selassie's inclusiveness. One of my more challenging speaking engagements at a maximum security facility was following a rousing speech by a Nation of Islam brother on the history of Haile Selassie and Marcus Garvey.

Mass incarceration is a huge problem in this country, especially for people of color—The New Jim Crow by Michele Alexander is a must read!—but inmates, stigmatized as they are, are just everyday people. The fact that they usually experience extreme difficulty finding work and housing after their release, makes the problem even more insane; it's too easy to go right back to prison, especially if you follow the example set by corporate America: to lie, cheat, and steal.

Recidivism for street criminals is a serious concern because of the lack of opportunity they face. The crazy part is that corporate criminals don't even face the same risk of incarceration as those who participate in street crime, even though corporate crime hurts so many more people. It turns out that the U.S. government actually defunded the pursuit of white collar crime when they embarked on the so-called drug war.

Working with inmates is so fulfilling because the need is so great. I've never experienced so much appreciation as when I've worked with inmates and even with the prison chaplains. The lack of connection between prisoners and the outside world is a huge part of recidivism and the desperation one can feel inside there—even for the people working there. One of the huge victories was when one of the inmates we worked with made it out and joined the board of the co-op I work for. Yes, he became my boss!

If you could shape prison reforms, what might they be? And can music, like in your case bringing in drums or bands like Niyorah and Bamboo Station, help pave a cultural rejuvenation behind bars?

Prisons need to be converted from literal hellholes and training camps for criminals to being incubators for creative innovation. There are so many quality people behind bars; with the right direction, these inmates could easily be our next leaders. And by creative innovation, I mean vocational and recreational, as both endeavors complement one another. Prisons should become farms, job training facilities for entrepreneurship, music schools, technical colleges, craft schools, yoga centers, et cetera. And instead of making pennies on the dollar, inmates should be able to make real wages. How else will those who don't know yet, learn the real value of an honest day's work?

While in college in Boston, you saw speeches by Abbie Hoffman and Bobby Seale, plus took a class by Noam Chomsky, not long after he had a split 7" with Bad Religion (*New World Order: War #1*), I assume. What were your impressions of Chomsky, and what learning moments stand out?

Actually, I took a class with Howard Zinn, and Chomsky was one of the speakers I saw, although I got to see him a few times. Those two were very different. You definitely needed some caffeine to make it through a Chomsky speech, but he was so eloquent when it came to giving a historical context to current events. He could cut through the bullshit like no other academic I've ever witnessed.

Howard Zinn, on the other hand, had so much energy. The class I took of his was on Socrates and Plato, and Zinn was a master of keeping it interesting. I think it could have easily gone the other way with just about any other professor at that school. He was so animated and excited about teaching, it was really infectious. And it wasn't lost on the other students. The class was packed! With the conservative administration at BU at the time—1988 or '89—Zinn was kind of a celebrity. He was a staunch adherent of the regular, albeit small, free speech rallies that were held on the quad, which Abbie Hoffman had come to. He was also probably the reason Bobby Seale came there.

When most people think of MOVE, they might recall the huge 1985 police assault that killed members in Philadelphia or the song "Operation: MOVE" by Leftover Crack. Knowing your own personal connection to the movement, how would you explain the group's philosophy to the uninformed, in terms of what inspires you?

To me, they were like an American version of Rastafari—only without the Bible, the focus on Haile Selassie, and without the herb. Most of the same ideas and approach were there: Ital (natural lifestyle); a focus on Africa as the birthplace of us all—members took the surname Africa, no matter their color; and being an active member of one's community, even though the approach might not have been "normal." MOVE's focus on stopping pollution and animal cruelty was way ahead of its time.

MOVE also had a very innovative approach—the strategy of John Africa—to taking on the criminal justice system. After members started getting locked up on a frequent basis, they came up with an idea that really worked. They had already been using "strategic profanity" as they called it—like it, or not—and would explain that it was the system that was profane, not the words people use. What was new was that they started deciding who would get arrested at each protest. Then at the hearing for their member who was charged, they would have ten or so members disrupt it. That meant the case got suspended, and then ten people were charged with contempt. So, one case would turn into eleven. They did this over and over until the city had to drop all their cases against MOVE because they just couldn't keep up.

Unfortunately, when the feds got involved, things got really ugly. And MOVE's intense radicalism was ramped up when a police officer trampled one of their newborn babies at a scuffle that occurred outside their residence. After the standoff in the Powelton Village, Philadelphia in 1978, they became international news because of the beating of Delbert Africa on TV. This was when the MOVE 9 was incarcerated—and they're still in there! Because their cases were so insanely skewed and the charges very likely false, MOVE was reborn in the '80s at a row house in West Philly. The result of their confrontation there was the famous bombing, and Ramona Africa was the only adult survivor. She was then incarcerated for rioting, if I remember correctly. She's the member I got to know in the '90s.

After she got out, we had something called the Beehive Collective in D.C., and we were running a free store, chapters of Food Not Bombs, the Anarchist Black Cross, and a punk record and zine store. We were also going to Mumia demonstrations regularly up in Philadelphia. This is how we met Ramona. It was striking how different she was than the idea you got from the mainstream media. You can go online right now, look at a Youtube video interview, and see how friendly and down-to-earth she is. And the demonstrations were so inclusive. Rather than controlling things, MOVE made it an open mic affair. Anyone could step up and speak.

Because of our relationship, we then set up speaking engagements for Ramona in D.C. and Baltimore, hosting her for half a week. At this time in my life, she and other MOVE members were such a big influence on me. By example, they taught me that you don't have to change yourself and suddenly try to conform to society if you want to have a family. In fact, it may be the most revolutionary thing you can do, to raise a family with activist values that include a respect for all life, as MOVE professed. I would say MOVE shepherded me into adulthood.

In 1989, Soulside was the first American band to play East Berlin and parts of Poland (UK Subs played there in 1983, Youth Brigade and DOA in 1984/1985) when the Berlin Wall was still intact. Did you feel like ambassadors of underground America? I understand Soulside might have inspired Solidarity Movement's push for independent media.

It was the folks in the punk scene there who brought us to Poland and who had taught the Solidarity Movement about techniques in indie media, specifically a fanzine called Antena Krzyku. Here's a quote from their Facebook page:

"Back in 1980's Antena Krzyku was one of the best known and the most important Polish underground zines created by our mutual friend Arek Marczynski. It was totally independent (which in late communist Poland also meant illegal) publication covering some aspects of independent music, counter culture and punk community on both sides of the Iron Curtain.

"Under Antena Krzyku umbrella Arek had developed also some other projects including: RED tapes label, Protekcja distro and booking agency, which became some sort of nucleus of Polish DIY community in the exciting era of changes in Central and Eastern Europe."

Our time there definitely upped the ante on what one could hope to experience on tour with a band. Going behind the Iron Curtain at that time meant you were walking into a completely different society from Western Europe and America. All they had there was traded only with the East—so no bananas in the markets, for example—and there were World War II-era bullet holes everywhere. In Poland, we played in cultural centers that looked like museums. At one outdoor venue, it was like the whole town came out to see us. We arrived a couple of weeks before the first free parliament election, which eventually brought the Solidarity movement to power, so it was a very pivotal time for them.

On the way to Poland, we played a totally illegal show in a Protestant church in East Berlin. It was something really special, as I was told, because punk rock was totally forbidden at that time in East Germany and a lot of punk kids suffered a lot under the Honecker regime. All in all, it was an experience I will never forget. It taught me the power of culture and connection, way before the internet. A similar circumstance was when Rain Like The Sound Of Trains played in a bomb shelter in Slovenia just after the war that split Yugoslavia apart. It was amazing to learn that it was a Food Not Bombs chapter over there that was feeding the refugees from the war.

I am sure the reunion shows will re-introduce the band to a wholly changed music scene in which money, technology, and networking tend to reign supreme—do you feel connected to the "now," or do you feel like you are fighting the good fight, but apart from the bustle of the music gristle?

Great question! To me, at this point, the only thing that feels different is that we are playing clubs instead of VFW halls or YMCAs. For that reason, it's harder to get an all-ages show going, but the feeling is very much the same. There's not that much money involved, and there's no big PR machine. It's people connecting around culture that they love and share. Even though the songs are at least twenty-five years old, the lyrics are still creepily relevant today, which I think is too bad. All the issues we were passionate about addressing that long ago are still around, if not worse. For that reason, it all feels very "now," but I will say it's been a long time since I've had an attentive crowd to talk about these issues with. I'm just pleased to be able to talk about their current context like Black Lives Matter and cooperative economics in between these hopefully not too timeless songs.

Soulside in Rockford, IL, 1988, by David Ensminger

Bobby in Tulsa, OK, 2015, by David Ensminger

RIP, Fred "Freak" Smith
Black Punk Pioneer

This tribute was originally published on-line by *Maximum Rocknroll* in Sept. 2017.

A week ago, a "semi-transient African American man" was found dead, killed from a knife wound behind the softball field of Las Palmas Park, located in San Fernando, CA. This was Fred "Freak" Smith, beloved guitarist who shaped the trajectory of mid-1980's punk in seminal bands like Beefeater, one of Washington D.C,.'s most inventive outfits. Having recently tried out for the band Romones, he had been living at Blake House, a group home, for a short stint, but wound up traversing the restless streets, seeking solace where he could.

For me, the legacy of Beefeater is summed up most forcefully in their brilliant, genre-blurring LP *House Burning Down*, released on Dischord after the band's demise in 1986. Combining hard funk, tribal stomp, raw jazz, shades of reggae, metallic leanings, and hardcore prowess, it's an unmatched landmark, even now. Yet, the band was unstable (drummers came and went) and their fiery brand of politics set the teeth of both right-wing and left-wing punks on edge.

Smith, who changed his name to Freak, was the nimble musical backbone of the band. After joining Strange Boutique, he also helped pave the path of elegant post-hardcore music in D.C. as well. In the last half decade, he shredded in American Corpse Flower. And wherever he went, he was described as vivacious, spirited, generous, and skilled to the core.

As Bobby Sullivan, singer of Soulside and Rain Like the Sound of Trains, texted me earlier today: "Fred Smith was/is a larger than life character who literally lit up my youth. As a young person immersed in the D.C. punk scene, I had an extra in: my older brother lived at Dischord House. That meant I saw many of these bands form, from first talking about it in the living room, to practicing in the basement, and then taking it to the stage. Onam (Tomas), the singer of Beefeater (Fred's band at the time) also lived at Dischord House, and I spent many mornings with him when I would sleep over. My brother was a late sleeper, so I'd end up in the kitchen getting breakfast together and chatting about all the things I wanted to bounce off my older brothers and sisters - all the fine folks on the Dischord roster in the eighties.

Fred was somewhat of an aberration in that crew. Unabashedly cussing, drinking, being himself with no fear of judgment, he was something to behold. He was also a very skilled musician bringing a different flavor to that scene, which was sorely needed. My most poignant memory of him was when my band Soulside played with Beefeater at D.C. Space, I'm guessing in 1985. Scott, our guitar player, asked if he could borrow Fred Marshall half-stack and Fred replied, 'Yeah mother fucker! And do what ever you have to do. Smash it if you need to!!!' We all knew he was serious because that's exactly the type of guy he was."

Other D.C. rockers like Jason Farrell of Swiz/Bluetip/Red Hare recall his outsized personality too. He emailed me this recollection:

"In 1984, I was a 14 year old little skater kid just starting to go to shows, meeting other skaters/hardcore kids, taking every opportunity to stage dive, reveling in this crazy scene we stumbled into. I didn't yet know much about the smaller D.C. bands that were percolating at the time (Rites of Spring,

Beefeater) because all my friends and I were focused on whatever Government Issue and Marginal Man were doing.

I'd seen Void a few times prior, but they didn't really click with me until this one Wilson Center show they were killing it. But apparently, it wasn't enough to satisfy this big black dude who kept screaming and heckling them from the pit."I better hear some motherfuckin' "My Rules!!!" Goddammit!!! If I don't hear "My Rules" in the next ten seconds I'm gonna kill every motherfucker ..." etc. It was kind of funny at first, but then it got kind of weird and a little scary.

After a few songs like this, the air was tense ...The singer seemed nervous. People didn't know how to react ... my little friends and I thought some shit was about to go down, and whatever it was would be beyond our capacity. But then they played "My Rules," the place exploded, and this crazy dude was overjoyed.

In the time since, I have convinced myself that this crazy man was Fred "Freak" Smith."

Our counterculture needs to reckon with the future. More and more legacy punks deserve attention and advocacy. I have personally seen medical issues sideswipe those I have been lucky enough to play alongside - like members of Mydolls, Anarchitex, Big Boys, the Dicks, the Nerves, and the Hates. Others, including Dave Dictor of MDC, have partnered with me on projects. But all have dealt with dire health issues. As punks age, they often feel economic duress quite intensely. While some cities like Austin and Denton (both in Texas) have set up some infrastructure and programs for musicians, much more needs to be done.

In addition, punks who are female, queer, people of color, and/or disabled (some prefer the term differently abled) are even more at risk, due to ongoing discrimination. Thus, those fighting for justice, equality, and fairness should not merely protest Trump's agenda, they need to react pro-actively to the issues affecting a growing segment of punk veterans struggling to pay bills, maintain homes and health, and stay free and productive.

Buying old records is not enough. Antifa is not enough. But each of us can change that.

This interview was originally published in a print version of *Maximumrocknroll* and the book *Left of the Dial* by PM Press.

Tell me about your musical heritage.

(Freak): In very early 1983, I had just quit my government job at the Department of H.U.D. My dad was one of the first black Deputy U.S. Marshals. My dad was a doo-wop singer in the 1950s with Marvin Gaye and Van McCoy. The band was called the Starlighters and had a hit song called "The Birdland." After they fizzled out, my dad got into law enforcement—the second generation of the Smith clan to do so. My mom was overseas working for the State Department (a gig she earned struggling in the ranks for at least fifteen or so years) while working for a 1960s program called "Voice Of America." They divorced in 1971. As my dad kept stressing me to go into law enforcement as a lifelong career, the music side of me was tearing me apart. So, I finally decided for the latter.

And you started to immerse yourself in punk music?

All this punk rock shit was happening in D.C. as well as New York, Massachusetts, Michigan, Ohio, and L.A. I was so intrigued. It was kind of like the Hippie movement of the early 1960s but more radical and more in your face—"We are sick of this shit world, and we are now here to fucking change it whether you fucking like it or not" attitude. In this circle of mostly pale, tattered clothing, safety-pinned boys, aside from the few black fans in the audience, there was us! Gary Miller, aka Dr. Know of the Bad Brains, John Bubba Dupree from Void, Stuart Casson of Red C and the Meatmen, and the late great David Byers of the Psychotics, Chucky Sluggo, HR, and myself. Now I am just noting the guitar players, but would never, ever, exclude or forget Shawn Brown from Dag Nasty, their first original singer, and the late Toni Young of Red C.

Through friends & some various acquaintances, more notably a guy named Ray Tony aka "Toast" and Eric Laqdemayo, aka Eric L from Red C, I heard about Madam's Organ and the Atlantis Club. Soon I was auditioning at old Dischord house for a band that, from the start, proclaimed, "We are not here to make any money, are you in?" My brother Big Myke said, "Fuck this" and split. I hung around. Beefeater had an amazing, but at any given time, a very tumultuous run, with two vegan, militant vegetarians and throughout the two and a half years of our existence, three meat eating, substance abusing alcohol driven drummers, and myself!

What was it like to be a black punk in D.C?

Let us all keep in mind that D.C. is what, 80 percent black, and this punk rock scene was fueled by angst-ridden white kids, a lot of whom I found out had fucking trust funds waiting for them when they became of legal adult age. Shit, I didn't even know what a fucking trust fund was back then. It was very strange to be these "token" Negros playing in front of predominantly all white audiences, but we did it. As Shawn Brown and myself will attest, there were fucking issues man. A lot of fucking issues that we had to address when we did shows. When I first heard someone refer to me as the "negro Lemmy," I was floored. I immediately lowered my mic stand down from the height that I set it. When I heard Shawn Brown being referred to as "the negro version of Ian MacKaye." I was floored again. When I told him, he was taken aback but still plugged on. In retrospect, even in this new scene, I was always wondering, would racism ever end?!

Most of us know you as Fred Smith, so tell me about the name change to Freak.

Like many blacks back then, through the 1930s until the early 1960s, a lot of fucking name changing went about due to many horrible scenarios always occurring in the segregated United States of America. I legally changed my name to "Freak" some odd years ago. My birth name, Frederick E. Smith Jr., is not my real name. My real last name is Ellis. When I found this out in 1980, I was horrified, shocked, saddened, and felt raped by both the world itself for letting me be born as a lie and my parents, who knew this shit but never told me until I was an adult. So not cool, man. There was some incident with one of my family members in the 1930s in another state, possibly a homicide. I really don't know. If this was the case at the time, I am very sure it was probably in self-defense against not getting lynched. My family keeps it very cryptic, but the truth was, this individual had to get out of town, disappear, and begin a new life. So, in doing so, the name was changed to "Smith." I have never tried to find our true lineage and probably never will. That would be too much of a strain for me right now and would probably just make me very, very fucking angry to find out all the lives I could've known all these years but didn't because of this incident. And a lot of other blacks will tell you I am not alone with this issue. So, changing my name finally gave me peace that I had been seeking for a very long time.

Being a drummer, I have to ask: why did Beefeater have three drummers, one for each recording?!

Beefeater had three drummers due to the fact that three drummers went through Beefeater. What I mean to say is basically guys came in and left for various reasons—theirs and ours. Bruce Atchley Taylor, our first, left due to the fact that his life was changing and he wanted not to tour. We were very ready to go out of town during the early stages. Mark Schellhaus, our youngest skinsman, was pretty much asked to leave by Doug and Tomas due to various addictions and attitudes at the time. I never got over that one. It was a band vote, and I was pretty much out-voted and pressured. If he wasn't out of it, the band would've ended, or at least gone on without the two of us. Again, that is a very painful part of the history of the band for me, and I am still not quite over it. Mark and I are still very close, and he took being asked to leave pretty cordially and just did so without much opposition. To this day, Mark is one of the coolest people I know—a very talented fucker like the rest of the other drummers. Again, it was a sad moment for me. Kenny Craun, Mark's replacement, and drummer number three, just came in and took us out thru the rest of our days and just went his own way to do other project when the band dissolved in 1986. Most notably with a punk outfit called the Rhythm Pigs, and he also hooked up with Chuck, Faith No More's first original singer. With bands, chemistry is vital, and for some reason, the boys, Tomas and Doug, were okay with Kenny. This was pretty unusual at the time for Ken was more of a rocker than a punk dude, but he had his style, and they really didn't buck at it much. The timing was funny, each drummer played on his own individual album, thus leaving his distinctive mark—funny.

"Need a Job" came out on Olive Tree Records, which a member of Lunchmeat described as "a shady short lived label, part of the HR (Bad Brains) Dave Byers crew . . . I doubt those tapes even exist." Everyone knows Dischord Records, but tell me about Olive Tree.

Hmm, for me, Need a Job is one of my favorites. The band was really getting out of the standard basic hardcore genre and were really starting to mix that genre with funk. On Plays for Lovers, the funk was there, but it was being played so fast that those grooves might have gotten lost in translation to some. It was being accepted by a new breed of hardcore punks actually hearing that fast groove, somewhat like the Big Boys were doing in Texas. Though the production for the Need a Job recording wasn't exactly what I was hoping for in a finished product, I was still glad the EP came out to show that we were growing as a band. As I remember, the actual Olive Tree label was established by some of the punk/rasta scene in D.C. Founding members of that label were Julie Byrd, Kenny Dread, and HR himself. Shady is a harsh word to describe the label, but . . . things sometimes did not happen in a timely and professional manner. Shit got done, but not without drama of some kind. Oh yeah, there are master tapes out there with shit still waiting, I hope, for life to the world. Everyone at Olive Tree just smoked too much pot sometimes. Not saying that liquor and drugs don't affect other aspects of labels and bands and the music scene, I am just stating a known fact, and as musicians we have all pretty much really been there.

When interviewed in MRR, the band listed people like the Isley Brothers, John Coltrane, and John Lee Hooker as influences. Is that why the band had such a melting pot sound—pulling from jazz, funk, and world music—because the band wasn't simply listening to Minor Threat records or mimicking 1977?

Fuck yeah, man. Beefeater, throughout its existence, listened to pretty much anything. We all were into our own worlds and brought them to the lab all the time. We took from this and that and just blended it into something. We fucking pulled from anything and everything. It was cool. Nothing was off limits. That is what made it cool. That is what kept things fresh. Yes, we were a hardcore band, in essence, but we had a lot more shit to experiment with, and we made damn sure we did. No restrictions.

I know Tomas was critical of go-go music (the genre of bands like Trouble Funk, who played with Minor Threat) because they often emphasized materialism (once called it "stupid music about dancing and being cool"). Do you feel he misjudged or misunderstood go-go music?

Tomas' judgment of the D.C. go-go scene was, in fact, his opinion. Whether it was a critical misjudgment of it, dunno. You would have to ask him. I couldn't stand the shit myself. Non-blacks have always loved grooves. It took forever for those to admit it, but they fucking love funk, soul, and grooves. I think at one time in the U.S., it was against the norm to reveal liking such music, but alas, times always change. Go-go to me was just a rip-off of bands that played stadium shows and gave the drummers a spotlight in the middle of the set. Go-go basically took that spotlight drum part and made it a one and a half hour-long song. Just basic jam sessions really, only highlighting a beat, the beat. Everything else—guitars, keyboards, etc. were put on the back shelf. The actual song was the beat. I didn't care for it, but tons of fuckers in D.C. and around the world loved it. How can a hundred Frenchmen be wrong?!

Looking back, the band is considered part of the Revolution Summer era, including Rites of Spring, Embrace, Marginal Man, Gray Matter, and others. Did you feel a kind of "movement" was happening, or is our notion of that time really a kind of myth making?

Probably about a good four years prior to me even joining Beefeater, I, in fact, was becoming, in essence, a fucking real punk rocker. Learning the values and creed of that phenomenon and adapting it to my lifestyle. Revolution Summer was fucking bad-ass and very, very real. I am so proud to say that I was a part of that shit, and it was no myth in any way, shape, or form. I remember us out there doing the Punk Percussion protests at the South African embassy and Reno Park shows and shows benefiting those privately funded organizations that actually help and make change for the good of the city's poor and under-privileged. That was a beautiful and awesome awakening for me in the punk rock world. All of us weren't fuck-up miscreants. We actually cared about real positive change, and we went out there to do it at any cost. Fucking cool man. Great memories there. And the bands and individuals who were out there with us at that time all have my sincere and undying respect. Again, when I say it was fucking cool man, it WAS fucking cool. I believe my friend Amy Pickering of Fire Party started the whole concept. Again, way cool.

For many on both the Left and Right, Beefeater was vexing. Obviously, the Right dismissed the vegetarian/environmental/ "political correctness" of the band, but even the Left was baffled by the anti-abortion stance of some members as well. What was your personal sense of politics at the time?

From day one, Beefeater was Doug and Tomas' vision, and it came with at least a couple of ground rules that the band stood for: vegetarianism/non-alcohol, environmentalism, and total political awareness and civil and human rights. No matter who was in the band at any given time, this message was creed. Now, with that in crystal clarity, Beefeater was comprised of four members struggling in groups of two. On one side, there was militant animals rights/ vegan/non- alcoholic activist fucks, and on the other alcohol drinking, women fucking, and at the time chemical experimenting, meat eating pariahs. As you can only imagine, this chemistry caused, on more than several occasions, problems. With most bands, this is usually considered a marriage, albeit ours was a very fucked-up, dysfunctional one, insanely. But we all definitely had no issues or disagreements regarding a woman's right to choose and gay and lesbian rights. At shows, we were always very vocal about what Beefeater stood for, even though at times you saw beers on a Marshall or near the drums. I know that was hard for Doug and Tomas, but they put up with it. But not for very long.

All the drummers and me tried our best to respect them and their messages as much as we could. It was hard considering our lifestyles and various vices at the time.

Supposedly, at your last show, which happened at Fender's (I once read), Gang Green played after Beefeater and were vocal about being anti-PC and anti-Beefeater. Do you feel that other punk bands were pretty hostile to the politics of Beefeater, or feel that the politics overshadowed the music?

Beefeater's last show was not at the Fender's Ballroom in Long Beach, California in 1986. I really don't know where that came from. As far as Gang Green is concerned, dissing us at that show after we opened for them and others, that was just a retaliation for an incident that happened early on that same tour in a different city in which the show was overbooked. They showed up and weren't allowed to play, and the promoter asked us to step in and talk to them about it. Not a good day for them at that time, but on the road shit happens. They said what they said, and so what? Gang Green is one of the great bands of the early and existing punk rock scene. I got no beef with those fun, crazy motherfuckers whatsoever. Shit, I used to work at the 9:30 Club in DC, as we all know, and those guys and me are all right. No issues at all. What was done was done. As far as bands hating our brand of politics on issues or whatever . . . shit! It just depended on what bill we were on, whomever that night was doing something totally stupid, like starting fights for no reason during our pits, racist skins sieg heiling us, dudes trying to get girls out of the pits, out of control bouncers, etc. Any form of bullshit we did not tolerate whatsoever, and we would stop performing at any given second until those issues were addressed by the crowd or the club. Whether the bands or fans gave us shit, we were able to handle anything. Not always contain it. But it got fucking dealt with as best we could. I believe our last show was in Washington D.C. in 1986. A sad show, but one that needed to happen so members could progress and move forward and still grow individually. Thankfully, everyone did.

I know Tomas has been critical of the punk scene, once telling a zine: "In a way they punks are society now too and that's a shame. They still buy 7-11 food; they have no impact on the government, or the economy. They still entertain themselves the same way, they have the same values and futures as everybody else . . . so there's no anarchy, rebellion there at all." Did you feel that punk represented an alternative society, or not?

If here ever was a true punk, Tomas Squip was one of those at the head of the pack, for real. Tomas really didn't give a shit about living beyond menial means—food, shelter, lifestyle. He lived at the Dischord House for a while in a room, shared a bathroom. He slept on the floor with no furniture. His pillow was a medium-sized rock and he had a blanket to cover himself. He was always reading and constantly on top of all the news, local and global, and on every political issue on the grid. That fucker probably doesn't even know it, but he taught me so much about the world, the system, and us as human beings. He really wondered why punks were doing the same things as everyone else did—get fucked-up, do stupid things, resulting in altercations with law enforcement, and not really trying to distinguish themselves from the norm they were rebelling against, other than clothing and music association. He wondered why people, including myself at the time, didn't try to alter their eating habits to respect animal rights, to change daily aspects of their lives to respect the earth, to be aware of things that are said at times that are racist and sexist and homophobic. He always thought a lot of punks weren't really trying to make change at all. No rebellion or real anarchy at all. It saddened him all the time. It was very tough for him. He really wondered if anyone, aside from a very small faction of the scene, were any kind of real alternative society at all! I thought it was definitely an alternative society then, and I still think so now. But then again, a lot of things would make an observer looking in totally disagree with me. Like everything else, it basically comes down to what a certain individual is going to do with it—with that punk rock ethic.

After joining Madhouse/Strange Boutique, one of your best stories involves Geordie from Killing Joke. What made that time period special?

I don't know if any of you really know this, but I must be one of a very minute number of the luckiest punk musicians that has actually had a very uplifting, incredible life through the various bands he's been in. Not only did I work at one of the country's top underground, cutting-edge clubs of all time, Nightclub 9:30 in Washington DC, I have also been in two very special bands that have allowed me to play with all of my peers for each band genre that I was in at the time and to excel at the music genre, whatever it was. In Beefeater, we were honored to play with such bands as Rites of Spring, DOA, NOFX, Agnostic Front, the Dickies, Scream, SSD, Dag Nasty, 7 Seconds, Bad Brains, Big Black, the Necros, HR, etc. As my run with hardcore came to its end in 1986, I was, in about four hours after leaving Beefeater, already enlisted in a now upcoming post-punk band—one more accessible than the hardcore scene and appealing to a more eclectic adult dance audience

Strange Boutique emerged out of the ashes of Madhouse, fronted by lead vocalist Monica Richards, formerly of D.C. punk band Hate from Ignorance. As my style was now changing to the heavily Euro pop indie sound, I was getting influences from the likes of the Cocteau Twins, the Damned, Killing Joke, PiL, Punishment of Luxury, the Slits, and Magazine. Unbeknown to me at the time, I would soon be touring with the likes of some of them as well. Fucking incredible, fuck, you couldn't make this shit up: this is a dream, right? Whaddya mean we are heading to England? For real? In fact, on a support gig with Killing Joke in England I was approached by one of my idols, the all-time European guitar great Geordie, during a sound check. He actually got to check me out and see what I was really about. I passed him in the corridor of the club, and he goes, "Mate you're a pretty good guitar player." I then asked, hey, would you put that down in writing for me?" He quickly responded in that heavy English accent, "No!" (laughing). Always magical when one of the greats takes even a little time out for the little guy. One of my best days of all time. Will never forget it. Wow.

For me, it makes sense, musically, since people like James Stevenson from Chelsea joined Gene Loves Jezebel, and New Model Army can be linked to the Crass scene. But why did Strange Boutique become such a good fit for you?

Strange Boutique took a real fucking gamble on me, really. Here I was this totally out of control hardcore guitarist, chains dangling from belts and shit, and they just took me in to play this new form of music I was coming into—dark, pop, heavy dance groove shit. After some early experimentation, we soon were labeled Goth. Now, at the time I was really growing. Unlike the days of Beefeater, I was now fully exploring new territories—new amps, effects (which I had never even considered ever using before in Beefeater), the now signature classic trademark Ovation acoustic/electric 12-string, which I learned to also send through the Marshall and JC-120 to run a solo thru once in awhile with full-on lead distortion. Strange Boutique was my time, and I was definitely ready. Probably to this date, even though my Blaxmyth did make a dent, Strange Boutique was and always will be the best band I have ever been in, period, fucking F.

BEEFEATER.

Oct. 31. 1984

at: King Kong's & SEX ON T.V.

$3.

Wed.

The "Death is Cool" Concert.

The Solution to the World's Problems

Minor Threat, Austin, TX, by Dixon Colbourn

Jeff Nelson from Minor Threat

Previously published in Artcore.

I have been reviewing *Dance of Days* and *Our Band Could be Your Life*, and have again felt that they miss a large chunk of the big picture, really relying on anecdote and gossip, it seems, more than anything, or small slivers. In fact, John Stabb told me that it's not the history he recalls. Do you feel these books, along with others like *American Hardcore*, HAVE done justice to punk history, as you know/experienced it?

I think some books have painted a more accurate, or more complete picture of certain parts of "the scene" than others, but then I also think it's ridiculous to expect a book to be able to possibly relay everyone's perspective. I think the chapter on Minor Threat in *Our Band Could Be Your Life* by Michael Azerrad is the best I have read for its accurate overview of things I personally was involved in. *Dance of Days* (Mark Andersen, Mark Jenkins) is good, but too long, and I find that an awful lot has been read into bands' and people's actions that I do not think necessarily existed. In other words, I think Mark is always looking for/hoping for a deeper meaning to everything, and not everything has a deeper meaning nor was everything motivated by noble purpose. Similarly, those people seen as insufficiently noble are castigated unfairly.

From the books' testimonies, plus from what I remember from Dischord mail orders of my own, the whole process was very DIY and hands-on, from folding lyric sheets to grabbing recycled boxes to hand-addressing labels for shipment, not to mention actually doing the mock-ups for covers. In essence, when you touched a Dischord product, the customr actually touched a living process, very grass-roots, almost touching the people. This certainly did not happen with large punk bands like the Dickies and the Clash, let alone stadium rockers. Is this the esential spirit of hardcore, even more important than the music in some cases?

I suspect that any homegrown operation, be it a band or a label, within any genre, has to start somewhere, doing things on the cheap. I think The Dickies and The Clash may well have been quite hands-on and thrifty and involved in the day-to-day efforts when they first started out, but upon signing to larger record labels that handled most things, and upon being confronted with a very busy schedule of shows, interviews, recording, realized they had to learn to delegate, and to concentrate on the things they thought were most important, i.e. the music. I tend to think that Hardcore punk is, for most people, an aggressive music that they find compelling at a certain age, and the importance they attach to the D.I.Y. Underpinnings of a band or a label is directly proportionate to their interest in/respect for things beyond the aggressive music. For some, therefore, the feeling of community derived from productive elements within a "scene" resonate strongly, and may mean as much as the music, while others may be just looking for a good time and could not care less about the efforts behind a show or a record.

I am struck how earlier you have mentioned that you felt that Fugazi and Positive Force, and even the concept of Revolution Summer, began to overshadow the sense of fun in the scene, even over-politicized punk rock. Yet, you did spend lots of hours, time, and money making 200-300 Meese is a Pig posters, and through an almost street guerilla-like operation, plaster the city, even across from his office. How do you square the two ideas?

I did the anti-Meese posters because my rage over Reagan, the Iran-Contra business, Oliver North, Attorney General Meese, and the NRA boiled over to the point where I felt I had to make the strongest public statement possible. A large poster was the only vehicle I could think of for my message - I knew I could produce it myself and get friends to help put them up. The whole operation was a wondeful collaborative effort, and I could not have printed all those posters nor put them all up without the help of many friends and many volunteers from Positive Force. If someone had at some point printed a poster with a message that I agreed with, and they wanted my help, I'd like to think I would have chipped in and helped them. But I think we all must pick our battles, and for me, there are WAY too many wrongs in the World to try to right all of them. I personally can only get involved deeply in political stuff when I really care about it, or get really angry about something: Meese posters, later fighting Oliver North when he ran for Senator in Virginia, and making large yard signs here in Toledo against the Iraq War and against Bush. I cannot immerse myself in political stuff all the time, or I get burned out. I felt (and still feel) that there are many in DC who fight every fight, and expend their energies trying to right every wrong. That is noble, but not for me. I feel that such an uber-awareness of injustices in the World can also lead to being a politically-correct party-pooper.

In the early days of of the DC punk and Dischord, was flyering a petty crime, like graffiti? Were there open spaces, like kiosks and stores (Yesterday and Today) available, or like many cities, was it controversial, meaning that many residents thought of it as an ugly, unwanted tainting of the streets? Did you see the act as furtive, edgy?

Putting up flyers was illegal. I cannot remember what the fine was. Certainly, some record stores would allow the posting of flyers, but in general, telephone poles were the #1 place to put up a Xeroxed flyer. For larger posters, it was harder to find spaces, and often signal control boxes at intersections were pasted over with posters and flyers. Some were more conscientious about it than others. I have always hated graffiti, and believe it harkens and hastens the decay of cities. I am sure many felt that our flyers and posters were no better. When wheat-pasting posters, I always made a point of NOT putting them on nice buildings, and tried to put them only where others had put up posters, such as on signal control boxes or plywood walls surrounding construction sites. The act of putting up a poster with wheat paste was far more brazen than stapling up flyers, and it felt increasingly risky to do so. I always envied Europe their large poster kiosks, specifically meant for the posting of bills.

Were kids openly participating in graffiti too, like in LA (Black Flag) and NYC (Sean Taggart)? I recall a photo by Tomas that he took of Scream featured on *Banging the Drum* in a room replete with graffiti, including several renditions of "resistance." Are you aware of where that might have been shot?

I suppose there were some kids doing graffiti, I don't really remember. In general, I think most of my peers in "the scene" were above the crude nature of graffiti. I know that Brendan Canty from Fugazi/Rites of Spring, etc., had a bedroom covered with graffiti when he was in the band Deadline and lived in his parents' house in D.C. I would guess it was something done sporadically by some, and outgrown. On the *Banging the Drum* record, which I just looked at, I do not see any graffiti on the walls behind anyone. I am guessing you are referring to the front cover itself, which featured a photo of Scream's bass player Skeeter, taken by Tomas. Tomas later wrote various things in the background around Skeeter.

I am always amazed looking at punk flyers because to me they really represent a break with the past -- products of self-taught, sometimes naïve, sometimes adeptly skilled artists -- that really look like nothing before them. They don't mirror boxing style rock'n'roll posters of the 50s, they don't mirror the organic curvy bright lines of psych posters, they seem to be a new language of rupture and roughness in places, and minimalism and almost pure utility in others. When making the flyers, did you have any antecedents in mind? Where did you get you clues from, the inspiration?

When I made flyers, I was just working with whatever images I could find, limited to magazines and such that you could cut up (only an asshole would cut something out of a book). Certainly, the hostage note graphics of the Sex Pistols were very inspirational, and the aggressive, crude-on-purpose nature of punk allowed one great freedom. I had been drawing logos of imaginary bands and beer cans for years, so things I came up with would have been the product of a 17 to 20-year old who was really just coming into a sense of style and layout. I would guess the precursors that come to mind for me (not as influences, but as predecessors) are Dada, and Russian Constructivist stuff. Certainly collage was an artform practiced by many in their scrapbooks, if not for public consumption. The Nation of Ulysses guys, Ian Svenonius in particular, was very much influenced by Russian Constructivist art.

Were people actively grabbing and trading flyers from all over even as early as 80-82? BYO would often insert a few flyers with every purchase, and people like Mike Muir from Suicidal Tendencies would use flyers to write on, as did many bands and fans. Did you find yourself trading and disseminating flyers beyond the time frame for a particular show?

Yes, people were collecting flyers from the very first day. Not as valuable things, but as art and mementos of shows. Also, the backs of old flyers were often used to lay out a new flyer. We would definitely send flyers to people who'd written a letter, and vice versa. When visiting another city, one of course tried to collect cool flyers. Some of us just kept more than others!

Minor Threat, Austin, TX, by Dixon Colbourn

Minor Threat, Austin, TX, by Dixon Colbourn

Living the Punk Ethic - A Conversation with Dischord Records and Fugazi Co-Founder Ian MacKaye

Originally published in Thirsty Ear, Dec. 2000, then re-published in my book Left of the Dial by PM Press.

While independent punk and alternative labels have flourished for the past two decades, Dischord Records, founded by Ian MacKaye and Jeff Nelson, is still indie music's most hallowed ground. For 20 years, the D.C. label, once a tiny operation that documented the music of a handful of friends, has grown to embody the principles of permanent rebellion, the seeds of which were sown during the stifling Reagan era. Throughout the 1980s, Dischord documented some of the most important bands in American punk: Faith (MacKaye's brother's band), which inspired both the Beastie Boys and Sonic Youth; Scream, a band that in one incarnation included Dave Grohl of Nirvana/Foo Fighters fame; Dag Nasty, whose guitarist Bran Baker is currently in Bad Religion; and Rites of Spring, whose core members -- Guy Picciotto and Brendan Canty -- became MacKaye's bandmates in Fugazi. Not only did the label provide a model, it provided a momentum, a burgeoning sense of possibility. Perhaps more importantly, MacKaye helped form Fugazi, punk's most beloved, respected, and tireless band. The band's front man traded in the punk anger that he forged in the outfits Teen Idles and Minor Threat for an "introspective, almost poetic vision, using abstractions in strongly structured compositions," in the words of Trouser Press. For nearly 15 years, the band has toured every corner of the globe, insisting that every show they play have a $5 admission and be open to all ages. The band has also sworn never to grant interviews to big corporate magazines, and they've turned down all the leviathans: Spin, Details, even Rolling Stone. In a bizarre turn of cultural events, Instrument, a video that documents a decade's worth of Fugazi concerts, practices, and portraits, was recently shown at the Museum of Modern Art in New York.

Is Dischord's 20th anniversary just another moment in the label?

I'm not nostalgic for the glory years, but at the same time I do think there's something significant. I like the idea that the label has been around for 20 years, because there's a gravity to it that's undeniable. From the very beginning, people were telling us that we wouldn't be able to do the label, that we'd have to move to New York City. They told us we wouldn't be able to do business the way we do. We don't use contracts. We don't follow any of the protocol that most people do. We questioned things. As it went along, people said we should copyright all these songs, and we said, why? What's the point? And we just asked questions, and did what made sense to us. People told us that we wouldn't be able to continue, but after 20 years I feel like, Wow, I guess we did continue, huh? When we get the 20th-anniversary release together the double-disc set should be available the time this issue hits the streets, I would like to draw a thread from the Teen Idles to whatever the latest band is. I would like to draw a thread, because I see a connection between them all. I know why every band is on the label, and I know the people in the bands, and that's important.

Dischord tried to keep prices down by printing "Don't Pay More Than $5" on the back of the records. But many merchants covered that up with their own price tags.

It's impossible to stop the prices in the free market. The idea was to put the mail order price on the outside of the record to create an option. You could get it for $5 postpaid from Dischord. Why pay more? Here's the address-mail order it. All you can do is offer up an alternative, and I never minded if stores charged a little extra because if someone wants the convenience of going down to the corner and buying it for a buck more, who cares? Occasionally, it was really, really abused -- people charging import prices because it said "Made in England" on the back or something. That happened. If somebody was really overcharging people, we would call them up and say they were out of line. You can't stop people; it's what the market will bear. It's a philosophy that I completely disagree with, but most of American business thrives on that.

You once said that you don't think anyone is going to change the world, but at least you want to live your life in the healthiest manner, with as much care, consideration, and love for people around you as possible.

Yeah, I still stand by that. There was a point when I felt that punk rock was all these people yelling about making life better, and part of what I thought making life better was about was being happy. I thought if you really wanted to reach that, then you should not just fight to be happy, but actually start allowing yourself to be happy. This is not a trivial thing. I'm not talking about having fun. Fuck fun. I'm not interested in fun. I'm talking about when people are fighting for happiness, or fighting to be free. Then I think that their biggest fight is sometimes with themselves. Today I was talking with a guy who thought that the fierce individualism of the punk community is what got in the way of the movement, in the way of things actually being mobilized, because people were so fiercely independent. He really firmly believed in collectives and formal cooperatives, but I completely disagree with him. I feel exactly the opposite. To me, it's the rigid codification of the formal collectives, cooperatives, and other groupings that get in the way of progress, because they have these rules, and nobody can break cadence. They can't get out of that, whereas individualists can. I was interviewed by a sociologist guy in 1983 for a documentary they were doing on the D.C. punk scene. Unfortunately, that whole project went up in flames because those guys ended up in a bitter quarrel, and they split the tapes up, and I think one guy destroyed all the tapes. It was a disaster. They videotaped all these interviews with my mom and dad, and all these other people. It was a huge project. And actually, the Minor Threat live video is a remnant of that. They did an interview with this professor who was a sociologist, and he watched an interview they shot of me, and he analyzed me, and he said I was a tragic figure that was going to be so bitter by the time I was 30.

Now you're 38 and pretty happy.

I think he can go fuck himself.

You've always been an entrepreneur, whether it was a comic book shop, or a skateboard place with Henry Rollins.

I'm always for some kind of social activity. I've always been up for building forts or making bike shops. As kids, we were up for whatever. I think it started really early on, the idea of building or doing things. Having a club, having a gang, just doing something that involved a companionship. Keep in mind, none of these things I did made money. Entrepreneurial suggests that I was always trying to make money. Actually, what I was interested in was construction work. I was into the idea of creating things. When I was 12 or 13, a lot of my friends started getting into drugs, and I just didn't. A lot of the people early on just tried to spend most of their time getting high. For me, that was so boring, because I just wanted to go do something. We got a day, so let's do something with it. Maybe their detachment heightened my sense of involvement.

There's a photo of you in the early 1980s at Dischord House with a Hendrix record, and it caused me, as a punk, to have a gestalt shift. I no longer had to be embarrassed about liking people like Janis Joplin.

She was a total inspiration for me because she put it out there in a hardcore way. When I was around 10 years old, I remember arguing with one of my older sisters about whether music could show somebody's emotions, and I was absolutely adamant that I could hear it in Hendrix. She was like, that's bullshit, but the idea that I could hear the emotion stuck with me for my whole life. To me, music has that. With Joplin, she was so powerful. I also feel Ted Nugent was naked in terms of his emotions. They weren't always pleasant, but he put them out there. Same thing with Joplin; she took a risk. It's not very often that people get to just go that hard. I'm 38 and totally happy to get onstage and just completely melt down.

You're the only person I've seen who consistently sweats through their pants onstage.

For me, that's a great gift in my life. It's not something that everybody-not that they want to-will try. But it's worth it. When I was in high school, I was skating, and skating is in part about the redefinition of life. When you're on a skateboard and everyone else sees sidewalks, I see runways.

Everything is an opportunity?

In high school I couldn't see how people were going to redefine themselves in terms of life. I was sure that it would all come clear to me, that there would be this underground, subculture movement that I would be involved with that would challenge conventional society, because I was not interested in becoming part of it. There was no way I was going to go to college. At one point I thought I was going to be killed by a car, and if I died, I didn't want to have spent most of my cognitive hours sitting in school. Basically, when I was in high school, the only rebellion I was seeing kids do was getting high.

Which is really non-rebellion.

Or anti-rebellion. The political kids, the yippie kids, were basically all stoners. Getting high was the one thing that anybody could do, but I didn't want to waste time. In the middle of all this, my friends started listening to punk rock, and I, at first, thought it was a dumb, junky thing. So we argued. And Nugent being the wild man that he was, and having seen his shows, which were so over the top, I couldn't believe that there was anything heavier. I remember getting in these polemic debates about 'Nuge versus the Ramones, really heavy arguments about what was what. In late 1978, I was given a stack of records.

The first Jam, the Clash.

All those records. I sat down and listened to them and became really intrigued, not necessarily liked them, but they scared me because it did not sound like rock & roll to me. They were challenging, like it was a whole new kind of music. The Ramones, at the beginning for me, sounded like a joke. Bubblegum.

You saw the Cramps early in their career, and it's a powerful memory.

It was something way deeper, and way darker. When I saw the Cramps in 1979, the room was packed with all different kinds of people, not just a room full of punk rockers, though there were punk rockers there of all shapes and sizes. The Bad Brains were there handing out flyers for their first show. There were junkie-type people, a huge political contingent, and these crazy redneck hillbilly punker-type kids. It was the first time since the radical 1960s-type stuff that I had seen people like this. And I said, here it is. This is what I'm looking for. It was the people who were on the margins of society, and that's where I always felt I belonged. There were people challenging political conventions, musical conventions, artistic conventions, sexual conventions, and psychological conventions. People were testing every water there was to be had. It was all there, and the show was a cathartic experience.

After your first band, the Teen Idles, broke up, why did you decide to document the band post-facto and create Dischord?

At the time, there were no labels that were interested in us, that's for sure. We knew that if we wanted to document it, we'd have to do it ourselves. Jeff and I are crazy about documentation. At the end of the day, we had made this tape and had the money. We felt the music was important and wanted to have a record of it. We had been a part of something that was really important to us. We totally believed in what we were doing, the punk rock or underground. We were like: this is our family, and we need to make a yearbook of this shit. While I think some of the music is great, I'm not saying everyone should like it. I could give a fuck. I mean, I'm happy if they do, but if they don't, that's fine. I'm not saying these are the best bands in the world. I will say that for me, it's some of the most important music.

What was the challenge for the label in terms of getting the records distributed?

I don' t think we ever really worried about that. We just made 'em and sold 'em. We never thought about it in terms of coverage. We just thought we'd make 1,000 records and try to sell them. We approached it more like a craft or a hobby. We didn't think, we're going on tour, we need to get those records in the store. We just thought we'd better make some records so we can sell them on the road. I don't think of records as promotional devices. At the time, if people got into punk rock, you quickly learned how to get the records. If you knew about punk rock and could buy a record, you could probably figure out how to get another one. That's also when mail order came into its own. Mail orders were so important for us, so strong at the beginning. We still have box after box of old mail orders. We didn't throw a lot of them away. So we still have mail orders from people who ended up being in bands later on. It's amazing.

What struck me back in the 1980s when I saw *Another State Of Mind*, **a film that features footage of Minor Threat, was the scene of you, energetic and polite, working at Haagen Dazs. Most people generally see punk rockers as shiftless, mindless, angst-ridden kids with pink mohawks begging for change.**

I always thought that was the media's version of it. I was faced with the same dilemmas as everybody, and I was dealing with reality. I wasn't squatting. I was doing the same thing as everybody else, just navigating it differently. At the beginning, we were taking an extreme position and rebelling, but we weren't rebelling in the way that the media would like us to rebel, which would suggest that all teenagers were idiots who just wanted to steal stuff and get high. But we were actually doing stuff. I had to pay rent and buy food. I wasn't dependent on anybody. I had no money. That's what always drove me so crazy when people accused us of being spoiled, rich white kids. It was insane. I was working three jobs at that point. When the tape was shot, I was working at Haagen Dazs, a movie theater, and driving a newspaper truck at night. Plus running the label, plus I was in a band, plus I was putting on shows, plus I was writing for a fanzine. I was going around the clock, but I was up for it. People say to me, it must be nice now. You're just living off the music. That's bullshit. It's what keeps me alive, but it's not what I'm living off of. I work my ass off all the time. I run the label, I run the band, I drive the van. We work on our own studio stuff, we are the lawyers, we are the managers. So it's not that our art is our meal ticket. We've always tried not to become too dependent on that. Chuck Dukowski from Black Flag said that he'd rather work a day job for the rest of his life than be dependent on his music for his living. That was in a *Damaged* magazine article called "Apocalypse Now." That quote fucking blew me away. It hit me exactly where I lived.

Who were some of your punk role models?

D.O.A. were in New York and wanted to play Washington. I told them the only thing going on was that we Teen Idles were playing this Valentine's dance at this high school. If you want to play, we'll put you on. And they came down and played this Valentine dance. We passed the hat, and they made, like, 30 bucks and stayed at my house. My mom made pancakes and stuff, and they were the greatest guys, and they were so psyched to play. To this day, I'm still an idealist because of that. To this day, I'm always up for a gig. I never blow off a gig. I can't believe when I hear about bands, particularly bands who align themselves with anything vaguely punk, that blow off a gig because they'd rather hang out in New York or something. Fuck that! If you commit to a gig, then you better do anything in your power to get there. That's just the way it is. We're so hardcore about that. Fugazi toured for ten years and cancelled only two or three shows ever, one because Guy was in the hospital and the other two because our van blew up. We physically couldn't make it to them. It wasn't until I was in the hospital in Australia in 1996 that we had to actually put down a string of dates.

But it wasn't necessarily about the shows or just about the bands. It was about the hang, about connecting with people.

Minor Threat, Austin, TX, by Dixon Colbourn

Fugazi by Chris Shary

To this day, I feel that way. The music is a thread or a currency. It's the center of attention, the point of gathering, maybe. My memories aren't really about standing there watching a band. It's always way more about sitting on a curb outside, or driving to the gig, or waiting in line. I have great memories of seeing the Ramones in 1979 in Virginia, a bit further out in the suburbs at a place run by the marines. It had almost a Hawaiian theme, an old-school bar/lounge kind of place, with cocktail waitresses and stuff. There was a huge line of people waiting to get in the show, and there was a skirmish at the front of the line, and the word spread like wildfire and came down the line that there was a dress code, and you couldn't have torn jeans. But you were going to see the Ramones. Everyone had torn jeans! It just rippled: Dress code, they won't let you in with torn jeans. Suddenly-it was in a little shopping mall-people made a beeline for the pharmacy and started buying needles and thread. There was a whole fucking parking lot of people sewing their jeans up trying to get in this gig. Fugazi tries to keep things interesting. We want to play the sock hops. One of the great aspects about booking your own band is the potential you might land in something weird. A person might call and say, do you want to play in an old circus tent? And most booking agents wouldn't necessarily feel that they could put a band in that kind of situation.

You have tried to play places that have a vaudeville feel to them, not the stereotypical big rock venues.

It's really one of the most frustrating aspects of music. It has become so difficult. You can't blame people for not wanting to rent their rooms to punk shows, because people have been so fucking disrespectful to property. Nothing used to make me more angry than people busting up bathrooms. I never understood that. I used to say onstage, "The toilet is our friend-it takes the shit away. So what the fuck is going on? Every show, you fucking idiots break the toilets. It doesn't make any sense." And in early D.C. punk, that was one of the strongest principles: Don't fuck up the room. And if there was ever an ass whuppin' to give, it was given to people who broke toilets and stuff. We'd just go after those people. It was not cool. We did not graffiti and we did not break windows. We were tough kids, and we'd definitely step up. There was definitely a lot of fighting going on. We understood that if we wanted the gigs to happen, we had to respect the venues-we couldn't fuck with them. Actually, I remember a turning point when people starting breaking things up, and it was really the end of the adventure of trying new places, because no one would ever give us a chance again.

In the '80s, the scene was very regionalized?

We were a D.C. label, and I saw things very regionally. That's what I thought was so cool about punk rock. I saw all these different towns had these scenes breaking out. They had their own bands, their own styles, their own way of dressing, even their own way of dancing. I could tell where someone was from by the way they danced. That was so cool, you know. The idea was, we've got D.C. covered, Alternative Tentacles had San Francisco, Touch and Go had the Midwest, SST was doing L.A. It was like, everyone do your own labels, and then we'll be a network. I thought everyone was just going to document their own scene. I thought that was the idea. But actually it turns out we're the only ones who ended up doing it. We still only put out D.C.-area bands.

Shudder to Think and Jawbox left Dischord for major labels, but the parting was amicable?

The bands are first; I still stand by that. Even recently, the Make-Up just went to K Records, and that's their decision. They're dear friends of mine. Good luck, but they're not on Dischord anymore. That's cool; that's the way it goes.

Why haven't bands on Dischord, with the exception of the Make-Up, released live records?

For the most part, the idea that you can capture a punk show on a record is an illusion. There are not many live great punk records. Fugazi had a really interesting conversation about live records because we tried to think of live records that are good that didn't have unreleased songs on them and weren't historical. In other words, Hendrix stuff is always historical, because he's obviously dead, so there's a historical notion to it. Well, we did live recordings, and they didn't sound any damn good. Bands were always out of tune, and the moment, what was going on in this room, couldn't be captured on a record.

So why pretend?

Right. The initial idea was to go into a studio and just record as live as possible. You have to understand, at least with Minor Threat's Out Of Step, the vocals are live. Everything was done live. I recorded Out Of Step standing in this little laundry room and just singing the lyrics next to a washing machine. It was one take. And I sang while they played. And if they fucked up, I just had to sing it again.

There's a lack of video footage as well.

I think we would have done video. It's just that nobody had the equipment. We couldn't afford it. Video cameras also seemed clunky at the time. Things are different, let me tell you. Now there's videotape everywhere of everything. But they haven't made the music good, I'll tell you that. Everyone is documenting every goddamn thing. The problem is now we have everything covered. Everyone knows how to do everything. They have distribution down, they got the labels down, they got the documentation down, and the only thing they've forgotten is that there's so few great songs. It's interesting because I've been asking a few people, who are the ones? In 1981, if you asked me, Jello Biafra, Dez Cadena, Joey Shithead, and, without a doubt, Jimmy Pursey these guys were visionaries. People like Penelope, these people were the fucking visionaries. All these people were like gods. I've asked a couple fanzine people, who are the visionaries now, the people who you just can't miss a gig? It's real interesting because I'm not getting a lot of answers. Some people say, Fugazi, you guys are a good band, a good find. But I know there are other bands that are decent. Yet there are very few people who say, that person, I cannot miss him. I'm curious. I'm always asking. I want to know. I listen to so much music that it's crazy. Today, I actually had somebody over and we listened to all these different new things, but also a Beach Boys bootleg, the first Queen record, and this human beat box guy.

Your partner Jeff Nelson is a completist?

Jeff is not really into any of the punk rock stuff at all now. He listens to country music, like you. We had an interesting conversation about that today, actually. He just doesn't feel a lot of connection to the punk stuff. He likes the older stuff, but with the newer stuff, he doesn't know what to make of it. It's tough, because I'm still very connected to a lot of bands, and would like to continue working on this stuff. It's an interesting time.

You've said that at some point the community you document will no longer

exist; and in a certain sense, neither will the label.

I like the idea of an ending. But, I mean, I've certainly underestimated the community because I didn't realize that it was a constant, steady changing of the guard. That people would keep coming along that I felt so connected to that picked it up and kept rolling with it, although it's certainly shrunk down quite a bit. I don't want to suggest that Dischord is the only arbiter of what's important. It's not. We just documented what we thought was important. At some point, it just stands to reason that our taste, or our view, is just not going to be able to take in what's important. We want other people to document what's important to them too.

You've said in interviews that for the most part, you don't have a problem with major labels. You've also said that you ultimately write songs because you want to say "Fuck you" to the music industry.

I think you're confusing that a bit. In the beginning it was like, the rock'n'roll industry, we're anti-that. We're punks. We try to operate outside of that system. That's not the reason we write the songs. But it is a nice effect of that.

Do you have problems with major record labels?

They're the musical manifestations of the corporate culture that we exist in, so I have a problem with them on that level. I don't think of them in the same way as oil companies. I certainly prefer DGC and Interscope over Northrop or Remington Arms manufacturer. I have much bigger problems with those companies and the pharmaceutical companies, which I feel have gone totally insane over profit. They are unethical, because they are not thinking about what's best for people and for life because it gets in the way of profit. Major labels' bottom line will always be profit, which is distasteful, but I don't lose sleep over them. They do what they do, and some of them do a fairly good job. They can basically take something that is pretty tepid and get millions of people to buy it. That's kind of impressive. People say, Jesus, these records are great because they're selling so many copies. Now, I don't have any documentation for this, but I think that for every wholesome soy burger/sandwich, there's been 500 Twinkies sold. People have said to me that Fugazi should have signed to a major label, because we would have reached so many more people, but I think that if we signed to a major label, we'd reach far fewer people because we would have broken up and not put out new records. With who we are, and the way we operate as people, I don't think we could have survived. It would have been too horrible to have been at the beck and call of those people. To feel that we were a point of investment, which bands are, basically.

You've also defended the notion of preaching to the converted.

People have used this preaching to the converted thing for so long as a sort of argument, as a kind of negative thing. It's not preaching to the converted that's important, it's what the converted do. I have no problem with preaching to the converted, because then the converted can go out and kick some ass. People try to dismiss you by saying you're just playing to your fans. Well, of course, that's what happens, that's why people come out to see you play. What's interesting is when you can make a moment happen, when you can take advantage of the great potential of having a crowd and music.

You have taken it to places like Chile.

We played fucking city parks in Hong Kong in the middle of the afternoon.

Those, I tell you, are not our converted flock. But by playing all these places, you just see yourselves better.

I remember you firing off a letter to *Flipside* when a girl took you to task on "Filler," a Minor Threat song. Do you take responsibility for things you have said?

To the degree that I can. I don't think I can ever reconcile or clear up the straight-edge stuff or the "Guilty Of Being White" stuff. Minor Threat inspired a subculture within punk known as straight-edge, which advocates abstaining from drugs and alcohol. Kids loyal to the trend would draw Xs on both hands with a black marker as a kind of counter-symbol to the marks underage kids receive at clubs that sell alcohol. A lot of those songs were written at a time when it never occurred to me that anybody outside my circle of 40 people would ever even hear the songs. You have to understand the context. Anybody who didn't grow up in Washington D.C. might have a little bit of a hard time understanding what "Guilty Of Being White" is all about. It's a little discouraging to be sort of heralded by Nazi Polish skinheads because they think "Guilty Of Being White" is such a great song, a great anthem for the white man. Knowing those lyrics are being posted on some Aryan Nation web site is discouraging, but life has that aspect to it. It's absurd. I never would have thought it. The same way, I think it's discouraging that there are kids cutting up other people for smoking cigarettes. That's totally ridiculous. If somebody is actually interested in my lyrics, I'm happy to explain what I intended. But I cannot control those lyrics. They're not mine. They're out there. That's the thing about sticking around—you continually have to answer for stuff. I recently got emailed from a kid maybe 15 years old giving me shit about something. On one hand, I'm like, Fuck you. What the fuck do you know? On the other hand, I'm kind of psyched that I have people writing me saying, Well, I understand that you guys are doing records through Caroline, they distribute records that are part of EMI all kinds of shit. But the fact that I respond, I love it. I'm still answering the fucking mail to this day. It's amazing to me. That's the punk thing. All the other people, the bands, my earliest peers, I know where a lot of them are, but they're certainly not singing in bands. They don't have to answer questions anymore. I see people and I tell them I still answer the mail. They can't believe it. They never answered the mail!

Even if it's troubling, it reinforces the idea that you have lived your life a certain way?

When I was in high school, I was not a good student per se. I wasn't getting good grades, and I didn't like doing book reports and shit like that. I didn't read the books, and I didn't do the homework. I wasn't interested in that stuff at all. I had to get good grades to the degree that I had to graduate. I did not want to fail. I was assigned *One Flew Over The Cuckoo's Nest* for a book report, or I chose it, and I had never read the book. I was trying to come up with something, because I suddenly had two days to do the book report. I was trying to read the book and trying to get through it, but I ended up calling Ken Kesey.

How the hell did you get Ken Kesey's phone number?

I called 555-1212 and asked for Ken Kesey's number in Oregon. His wife answers the phone. He's out of town. But she talked to me for, like, 45 minutes about the book and what his ideas were. Not only did I immediately write a report and get an A on it, but I fucking read the book because I couldn't believe she had been so kind to me. I'm doing book reports all the time now. Kids are always calling me about shit. I'm always happy to talk to them.

MINOR THREAT

minor threat

WITH THE UNTOUCHABLES

+ S.O.A.

AND BAD BRAINS

...and more

BEST ON?

Sat., Dec. 13th BENEFIT FOR PAUL'S AMP $2 AND AT

1929 CALVERT ST.

d.c. space 7th & E nw

DEC. 17th and 18th

UNHEARD MUSIC FESTIVAL

nurses

untouchables   type 'o'

S.O.A.   half japanes

g.j's   wiggly mitter

fluffy Pig

and more.

The SA 12 Riot Helmet is specially designed for use by riot squads. Manufactured from polycarbonate and lined with shock absorbing polystyrene – SA12 helmets will resist blows of up to 90ft lbs., normally fatal. An acidproof, fireproof and splinter resistant visor is also supplied.

SA121 Shockstick. A protective electric baton for riot control or personal protection. The shockstick utilises penlight batteries and can deliver an electric shock equivalent to 6,000 volts but with minimal amp rating, thus causing no harm or injury.

BY ED COLVER

Ian MacKaye, Minor Threat by Ed Colver

Minor Threat by Ed Colver

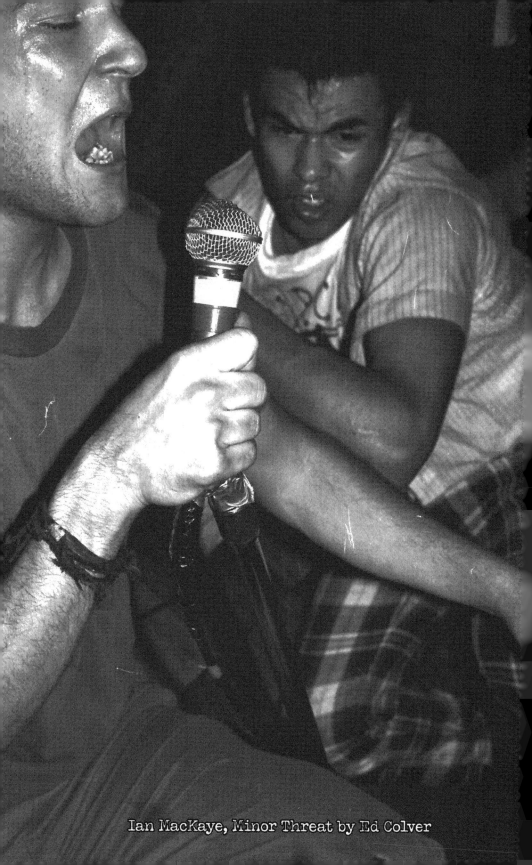

Ian MacKaye, Minor Threat by Ed Colver

Lyle Preslar, Minor Threat by Ed Colver

Brian Baker, Minor Threat by Ed Colver

Jeff Nelson, Minor Threat by Ed Colver

Ian MacKaye, Minor Threat by Ed Colver

Minor Threat by Ed Colver

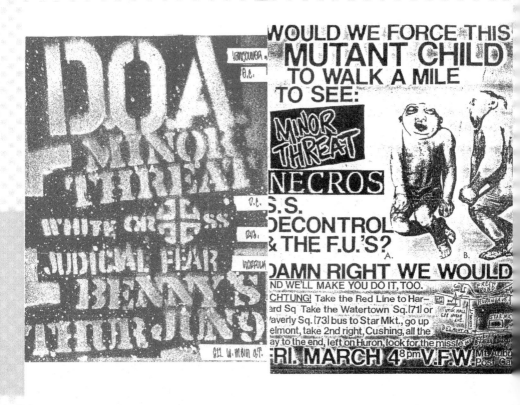

WOULD WE FORCE THIS
MUTANT CHILD
TO WALK A MILE
TO SEE:

MINOR THREAT
NECROS
S.S.
DECONTROL
& THE F.U.'S?

DAMN RIGHT WE WOULD
AND WE'LL MAKE YOU DO IT, TOO.
ACHTUNG! Take the Red Line to Har-
vard Sq. Take the Watertown Sq. [71] or
Waverly Sq. [73] bus to Star Mkt., go up
Belmont, take 2nd right, Cushing, all the
way to the end, left on Huron, look for the missile
FRI. MARCH 4 8PM **V.F.W.** Mt. Aubon Post Car

MINOR THREAT
FROM
D.C.

APRIL
30

WITH

AND

THE
FLESH
COLUMN

SERBIAN
CHURCH
HALL

MINOR THREAT
LOS POPULAROS
CIVIL DEATH
CONFLICT

Tuesday 29
March
BACKSTAGE
321 N. 4th. AVE.

JANUARY 26, 1989

FUGAZI
ULYSSES
JACKHAMMER
ORCHESTRA
930 CLUB
$5.00 9:00 PM

ALL AGES

A.S. Program Board & KCSB presents

FUGAZI
FUGAZI
FUGAZI
FUGAZI

BEAT HAPPENNING

The Pub **downcast** $5

Friday May 18, 8:00 pm

tickets available at A.S. ticket office, Rock House, Morning Glory & Sound Factory

FeEd THe hUnGrY

Soulside,
the Hated
Thorns
Fugazi

$$$$$$$$$$$$$$$$$$$$$$$$$
THURSDAY, DEC. 3, 1987 FIVE DOLLARS
7:30 PM
WILSON CENTER (15th and #3#3#3
Irving Sts., NW)
Y?Y?Y?Y?Y?Y?Y?Y?Y?Y???

you don't rise
when people fall

SPONSORED By POSITIVE FORCE D.C.

BENEFIT FOR THE COMMUNITY FOR CREATIVE NON-VIOLENCE(CCNV)
FOR USE IN ITS EFFORTS TO FEED, CLOTHE AND GAIN JUSTICE
FOR THE HOMELESS AND POOR OF WASHINGTON D.C...; YES, YOU
TOO CAN HELP IN THIS STRUGGLE...INFO, CALL 276-9768;;THANX

ROCK 'N' ROLL!
benefit for sexually abused...
Kids! (heartly house)

FROM D.C.
FUGAZI
w/ ian mackaye...dischord

FROM D.C.
3 (THREE)
w/ jeff nelson... minor threat

& local band
SecoND NaTuRe

tickers: S.N.
waxie maxies
weinberg

7:30 PM
WED.
NOV. 25TH

AT THE **weinberg center**
20 w. Patrick st.
frederick
$5.00 (301)694 8585...info

UNION FOR CHILDRENS RIGHTS

FUGAZI
OFFSPRING & 411
ONE NIGHT ONLY AT THE
HOLLYWOOD PALADIUM
SUNDAY SEPT. 8
ONLY SIX DOLLARS

GOLDENVOICE

TICKETMASTER
MAY COMPANY & MUSIC PLUS
(213) 480-3232 · (714) 740-2000
(805) 583-8700 · (818) 276-TIXS

NEMESIS

When I hear the word **culture** I take out my checkbook

Positive Force DC presents:

The DC Underground Invitational

with

Fugazi

The Vertebrates

7pm Monday, August 7
Fort Reno Park
(Wisconsin and Chesapeake Ave., NW
near Tenleytown Metro)

All expressions rising out of a grassroots dissident culture of compassion, creativity, and resistance are invited to publicize themselves at this event. This means activist groups, art, fanzines, CD/record/tape labels and probably many other possibilities we haven't even thought of... the more the merrier! Table space will be provided. One request, however: since the selling of merchandise is prohibited on National Park land, please don't sell anything...or do so with a very low profile, and at your own risk. In other words, *bring it all on* but leave the checkbook at home! Thanks...and for more information on this event or on Positive Force, call 703-276-9768. Spread the word, OK?

Shudder to Think - Late 1990s, Live at Fitzgeralds, Houston TX

Editor's Note: This is a long lost, unpublished review left for twenty years, for better or worse, in a box. I have since grown to appreciate late-period Shudder to Think, but I do believe this text offers a glimpse of my grappling with the band's mutations, perhaps felt by others that gravitated to their earlier gigs too.

When Shudder to Think played in Houston last night, they were languid heroes, ebullient, possessed by their own ability to catch a slanted effusive phrase and plunder it over ebbing guitar licks. They are a clash between form and non-form, sweetness and melancholy, memory and desire, excess and simplicity. At least they used to be. That much seems to be changing.

Listening to them in 1989 was like looking at a Jackson Pollock painting for the first time. The rabid painter liquidated representational figures in favor of pure motion, thick muscled swoops of paint, and self-contained myth. Shudder's music was slightly akin to this. Their music huddled in my psyche like an erotic hallucination disturbed by caterwauling vocals and tense haywire guitar. Their songs always felt sculptural, like works in progress melting in front of you.

They didn't rely on conventions of late 1980's by-the-numbers punk. They expand, fall back on themselves, reinvent and mutate the punk ideal form. They took a high soprano voice, drove the free-association flowing vocals into a bulldozer guitar, then added a steady streamlined bass beat to make it slightly smoother on the ears.

It amounted to a partial solution to the dullness and ennui that overcame post-hardcore bands turned indie rock idols like the Lemonheads and Dinosaur Jr. While those bands swallowed MTV wholesale and quickly became taxidermized, Shudder swooped and stamped their blood into our chemistries. Unfortunately, most of that spell has worn off like an old wax job. Memories flake away: signs of musical duration and succession begin to flicker and fade.

In literal terms, they are half the band they used to be. Guitarist Nathan Larson jumped ship from Swiz a few years back, while new drummer Kevin March hails from the equally cool Dambuilders. Since Shudder re-grouped for their first major label outing, they seem to welcome retooling but lose aspects of their shimmering, mesmerizing power.

Their new songs, and re-makes culled from the old catalog, are oddly clinical, slightly humdrum, and quaint rather than queer. They're not so much slickened by studio excess as they are simply lacking in spinal electricity.

When I first saw them in Rockford, IL at the suffocating late-summer Polish Falcon's Club, opening for headliners SNFU, circa 1988, they were transcendent. In fact, there were rough, breathless, and sacrosanct simultaneously. Abrupt and abrasive, they offered a fantastical bombardment.

The singer wore a thin white T-shirt draped over his lean edgy shoulders. His flaxen hair flopped down from a broad forehead into mussed curls. Cut-off jeans snagged his crotch, exposing lily-white legs. It was surreal.

The skinheads went into a half-baked stupor. They didn't know what to do -- just point, gag, maybe secretly buck their bony hips. Shudder to Think kept cranking and spinning weird narrative hi-jinxes on top of the dread-locked guitarist's scratchy finger probes.

Now older, in a brief glammy limelight, dressed for small success, they radiated much dimmer. When they reached back for an old prowling Dischord tune, it was more like art-drenched, slightly bubblegum-meets-glam undertows, and deconstructed pop. It stuck to the ear temporarily, soon awash in its own unstirring sonic loam. They are just hamstrung, more buttoned up: the prowess of "Call of the Playground" is no feral "It Was Arson" or spare and limber "Corner of My Eye."

Seeing them undulate and engross themselves, I smiled, knowing they are brief anti-heroes of what is otherwise often staid alternative music, but they are no longer resplendent, reverberating revolutionaries. Sure, I suppose they have spiraled towards maturity, but I like their naive apprentice punk, when being atavistic and shambolic meant everything. In 1988, I felt Shudder was on the verge of becoming ever new, ever potent.

Yes, they remain fluid, high styled, full of stretched syntactical wit and ploy, but the fever dream has been tamed and tethered.

Shudder to Think by Chris Shary

Fire Party - An excerpt from Women in Punk

As Revolution Summer faded and Dischord bands took a new path in the post-hardcore era, Fire Party helped define the gestalt and the power, joining the likes of mid-period Scream as well as Fidelity Jones, Shudder to Think, and 3 to show how punk's earnestness, guitar-thronged maturity, and sense of abstract poetics (paving the way for Jawbox) could enthrall. Not as heavy and metallish as L7, nonetheless the band could grind with a groove, anchored by the rollicking bass of Kate Samworth and powerful drumming of Nicky Thomas on tunes like "Make It Quick."

Plus, the vocals of singer Amy Pickering could shift, within seconds, from a mellow lull to a shriek that could shatter a stormy sky to a boundless Whitmanesque roar. At her fiercest, on tracks like "Bite," backed by insistent drums, she whips up a kind of punk Janis Joplin, though the blues swagger is transformed into punk insistence. "Just bite it off and chew your way through," she cajoles with throat-burning, raspy intensity. Musical moments of "First Course" feel faintly like Joy Division (just listen to the spare, all-alone drums at the end - detect the slight echoes of "She's Lost Control") enforced by the quintessential feeling of emptiness, uncertainty, and purposelessness.

Yet, the mere guts and stamina embedded in Pickering's voice proves that the reason people sing about gray modes is to actually reinforce the will to live. One must taste of a bit of the void, the strain of feeling at wit's end, in order to understand how to settle back into the arms of life, and be smarter, bolder.

"I don't want to hide any longer behind anger and pain," she avows on "Prisoner," easily one of their toughest cuts, which plows ahead as Pickering seems to deconstruct the nature of living in public -- full and honest -- even as people prod into lives, causing anyone to desire a degree of evasion. It's a barn burner that is relentless and unchained. The same might be said for "Only Nine Mottos," a two-minute torch that is self-reflexive and a bit meta-critical: Pickering tackles songwriting itself, all while recognizing that, unlike first thought best thought, often "...first comprehension isn't what frees."

Perhaps it's more like the act of seeing, and re-seeing, writing and re-writing; meanwhile, the very act of writing about music, the sometimes wanna-be intellectual efforts of people like me, may be like turning an artist "inside out - then we can see what's really me." Perhaps that offers pure irony - reviewers think they can shine a transparent light on writers, but the actual slippery sense of self, the shifting person behind the song, will always elude. Words fail to deliver certainty, alas, on both sides of the process - both song and commentary.

Above all, above the band's throbbing din, its weaving and tilting rock'n'roll sensibilities, and its soluble intensity, Pickering is the poet at the heart of it all - reaching out to Rainer Maria Rilke on "Engine," searching for modes of control and contentment on "Cake," tearing apart the notion of luck and desire on "Basis," as well as dealing with the compulsive, omnivorous need for space and breathing room on "Drowning Intentions." That tune seems to suggest that the walls people construct—self-imposed boundaries - keep people negotiating how much they are willing to share, perhaps suffer, as people impose their wills (even in kindness) upon each other. Hence, these tendencies end up molding the kinds of relationships that never quite satisfy.

In the end, perhaps all people have is an unstable image of each other, Pickering infers, I think. Luckily, the music is a well-shaped maelstrom that keeps all these thoughts from being too ponderous. Pickering is at the helm, the guide to an inner-country, never flummoxed to a point of paralysis. Freedom is always ticking under her breaths, and still is, for she has become a fervid outdoors climber, hiker, and photographer, always seeking the lone, difficult stretches that make life seem more spontaneous and spirited.

Fire Party by Chris Shary

An interview with Scott "Wino" Weinrich, former lead singer for The Obsessed and St. Vitus, and current leader of Spirit Caravan

Originally printed in Left of the Dial No. 2, 2002.

Wino was always a rocker. It's almost as if childhood avoided him, or he was born in a cocoon stuffed with old Stooges, Sabbath, and Marc Bolan records. He made punks sway to his metal onslaught during the salad days of harDCore, hitched a ride on a bus known as St. Vitus during the dog days of SST, reformed the Obsessed and flirted with major label meltdown, kicked a habit or two, and re-ignited a friendship with Joe Lally from Fugazi, whose label Tolotta offers America the drenched sledgehammer rock of Spirit Caravan. Wino is an archeologist of heaviness, so why mess around with the surplus of dredged up schlock like Staind and Slipknot when you can have a baptism of hot molten Wino?

In many interviews you have described seeing Black Sabbath as a 12 year as an incredible moment, and it's obvious that it has influenced your music, but what about seeing the James Gang at age 11?

The James Gang are still one of my favorite bands, though I do have to say that the James Gang I saw was fresh after Joe Walsh had just left, so I didn't get to see the Joe Walsh James Gang unfortunately. But the version I saw was The *Straight Shooter* band. I don't know if you are familiar with that album.

No.

"Straight Shooter" is when they got this guy Dominic T to play guitar, a Canadian session guy. Later on he did *Miami Vice* and shit like that, but he was an amazing fucking guitar player. When I was 9 and 10, I used to go into the pizza joint and "Funk 49" was on the jukebox, and when I was 9 or 10, that was my favorite song. The guitar on that is amazing till this day. Everybody used to play "Funk 49" wrong, like every guitar player would try and play that song but they'd play it wrong. One dude finally showed me that part that goes ... I've even seen Tommy Bolin videos when he was in the James Gang and he'd play it wrong. When I went to see the James Gang it was my very first live show. It was at this weird venue Shady Grove in the Round, and the stage was in the round and it was one of those that would slowly turn. So that was pretty wild.

You went with older an older brother or sister?

Actually, I had an older friend, my neighbor. She was considerably older than me, seven years older, and she was pretty instrumental in turning me on to lots of stuff. She was an enormous Allman Brothers fan, so she turned me on to the Allman Bros.

You loved the Beatles partly because they were heavy and partly because they had a dark side.

I'm talking about "Happiness is a Warm Gun", and I'm talking about some of the stuff off of *Yellow Submarine*, like "Only a Northern Song". But what I also mean by darker is "In My Life", that kind of stuff. What I kind of meant was a non-happy kind of sound, like a melancholy sound. A lot of their songs could be a little bit gloomy to me. That's why I liked them. I was never a big fan of the really happy-go-lucky stuff, the Paul McCartney stuff, the "When I'm 64"

shit. I mean I appreciate the genius behind it, but it wasn't my favorite stuff. The George Harrison songs, stuff like "While My Guitar Gently Weeps", c'mon, that's not a happy song. I don't think so.

The song has a density to it also.

It's got a density. Like when I first heard the Plastic Ono Band's "Cold Turkey". That was a little post-Beatles, and I'm talking about the "Cold Turkey" single version, with Clapton on guitar. The totally raunchy fucking guitar. That was classic Ono Band. I was like into all the Beatles stuff.

Were you hearing this on FM radio, alongside Mahavishnu Orchestra?

I had Beatles records. The Beatles were the Beatles and I was 12 years old in 1972. And I was into the Monkees. The Beatles were a mainstream band. That was an easy band to be into when you were young.

But were you popping into record stores at age 12?

By age 12 I had already changed. I was into the Beatles from 7 on. I was into them in 1969. They were influential. I listened to the White Album all the way up, like that song "Julia". I started getting into Sabbath and Hendrix kind of at the same time. Then I discovered Mahavishnu. But I have to tell you, since you're from Texas, that one of the turning points in my life was hearing Roky Erickson doing "Two Headed Dog (Red Temple Prayer)". I'm a big Rocky fan. I had always wanted to learn more about the 13th Floor Elevators because of that one song. It's one of the first totally obscure rock songs I heard on the radio, and it made me realize that hey, there's more out there.

Back in the days of FM when they would play deep cuts from the records, not just the singles.

Even into my teen years, believe it or not, there was a great radio station at one of the universities around here. At Georgetown University, which I think, if I'm not mistaken, is a Catholic university. There was a radical radio station at the university that had a very limited broadcast range, but I was lucky enough to get it where I lived. I remember they played the entire record of Budgie's In For The Kill. How off is that? I thought that was weird back then when I was fifteen.

Do you remember listening to it straight through?

Well, I was doing something very memorable at the time. I was actually in the back seat of a Cadillac.

You got into some trouble as a teenager, and became ward of the state?

I became ward of the court.

Was music some kind of safety net that you could fall into?

Music was totally there for me, a special place for me, even when I was locked up. I was a really big Zeppelin fan at the time, so especially songs like "The Rover" would do it for me. It would give me a thrill. I remember I had just gotten Physical Graffiti right around those times. I was real into the stuff, and was a major Jimmy Page fan. That stuff would get me through. I was still writing songs. I don't know if you are familiar with the Obsessed, but we did a song called "Freedom". Well, I wrote that song because I actually knew I was about to be incarcerated, and I was very angry.

When did punk music begin speaking to you?

I was always into high energy music anyway. Before the punk thing happened I was already into the Stooges and the MC5. I was familiar with "Raw Power" way before the Pistols and all that. We were listening to the Dictators. We had them all. I had "Go Girl Crazy" and "Manifest Destiny." When "Blood Brothers" came out it practically blew our mind. It's the quintessential fucking rock record. So we were already into the Dictators then discovered that Australian band the Saints. We had I'm Stranded, which I thought was okay, then Eternally Yours came out, which was a much better record. We were into Radio Birdman, the Saints, all that kind of stuff. Then of course the Pistols happened, who I dug, because I really dug that record. It's a rock'n'roll record. The sound is rock'n'roll. Of course, you have Johnny Rotten with his lyrics. I think that everybody felt the energy with the punk thing because people were pissed off. Of course, the kids in England had it a lot worse than the kids in America, but the kids in America appreciated the anger too. Right around that time, the Bad Brains started doing their thing. The Bad Brains were a fusion band from a bad part of the world out here. They started off in Prince George's County, which is really known for being a really rough police kind of county, with a lot of low income folks being brutalized by the cops all the time. The Bad Brains were basically these pot smokers and low life that never cut their lawn and lived in Prince George's County and played fusion. I have some really early Bad Brains stuff, and they're playing a song called "Redbone in the City", which is a total take on "God Save the Queen." They went radically from this progressive fusion band, to kind of imitating the Pistols a bit, then they realized that they needed to combine the energy of their fusion stuff with a dramatic punk delivery, so that became the Brains that we all know and love. Void was happening, Minor Threat was happening. I got a chance to see all that stuff first hand.

Your band the Obsessed guys were considered the Motorhead of the DC scene, metal guys who were respected by punks. Maybe even a bit like Thin Lizzy too, who the UK punks seemed to like.

I got to tell you though. A lot of people I know are head over heels Thin Lizzy fans, but don't like that sappy, sweet shit. On every record that they did there's so much bullshit you have to wade through to get to the meat. That's how I feel. Phil-- is a ballad writer, basically.

The first couple of records were very prog rock.

Well, of course Gary Moore's first band, the original Skid Row, were an Irish prog band. The original Skid Row, that's some rare shit. Anyways, having that comparison is interesting to me. Basically it took us awhile to win the punks over. We had a singer for awhile who was kind of a punk singer, and he was way ahead of his time. He was always telling me to do this or that, and he was the guy who got me to change my long hippie hair style into a more modern cut. He had this cut off leather jacket and this leopard skin bandana way before Stiv Bators. We played shows opening for the re-formed Dead Boys.

How were those shows?

They were pretty radical because we still weren't 100 percent accepted by the punks back then. They loved our originals, but they hated the fact that we played punk rock covers. We were kind of outcasts then, although we had a big suburban following who would come to these shows downtown with all these punks. So the crowds would pretty much clash. Once we canned our lead singer, and went down to a three piece and played all originals, that's when Iron Cross started liking us and playing shows with us. That's when I became friends with John Stabb and we played with Government Issue. That was when Ian started paying attention.

Once you went out West and started singing for St. Vitus, did you have to win over audiences much like you did in D.C.?

It was hard man, it was hard. It was hard going. We played really small shows. I missed touring with Black Flag. Before I joined St. Vitus, they toured with Black Flag. I wasn't there for that, but I joined soon after. Our first tour we did was with the Mentors in 1987, and those shows were pretty big. But no one knew who we were, but we were fucking kicking ass. But it was weird, because no one knew who the fuck we were. The record with me on it wasn't out yet, but they had had a couple of albums, but it still was a total struggle on the way up until Born Too Late, when we got our first overture from Europe.

The label Hellhound from Germany?

Yeah, they wanted to bring us over. We had a little following over there. When we first went over to Europe that's when we realized that there was life out there, that people were into St. Vitus. We were actually doing some pretty big shows.

Later on with the re-formed Obsessed, you played a crazy big show in Denmark?

85,000 people.

Did that blow your mind?

Yeah, it blew my mind, but it was also incredible because it was one of those picture perfect gigs. You were set up for all kinds of nightmares because the thing was so big. We had a soundman with us because we were on tour at the time. Basically, we had a picture perfect set. It couldn't get any fucking better. I had perfect sound on stage. I was like a mile away from everybody up there, but could hear perfectly. We were really in tune, and everything was groovy. It was one of those magical shows. I saw Kyuss later on that day have a terrible show, basically fold after about three songs.

What about Danzig and Prong?

Prong got the power shut off on them. Danzig was a real prick. You have to remember that it's a festival. So there's 30 or 40 bands each day. They had these auxiliary classroom type buildings set up for dressing rooms, so everybody had their own dressing room. Danzig had his own private dressing room, but had his thugs go back one point during the show way before he even played and made everybody leave their dressing rooms, and cleared out all these bands' dressing rooms, and never used them. We were told, "you have to get the fuck out." And they stayed empty. He was such a prick. People started leaving when he was playing, and they shut the power off on him because he played too long. He is just a cock.

Were you into the Misfits and Samhain?

GOVERNMENT ISSUE
IRON CROSS
the OBSESSED

SAT. FEBRUARY 25
AT GLENMONT REC. CENTER
(ON RANDOLPH RD. / NEXT TO WHEATON
HIGH SCHOOL) **7:00 PM** only **$5**

I was really into the Misfits more than Samhain, but then I had an opportunity to meet him at an early show with the Meatmen. The Obsessed played with Tesco Vee in New York City at some club, and of course, we were hated by the punks. Danzig put on the show. He and Brain Baker, they were just cocks together. Brian is one of the most arrogant people you could meet, and he'll deny his whole role in Junkyard.

Now the critics call St.Vitus seminal and prophetic, but why did it fly over people's heads at the time?

That's a really good question. I don't know why that is, maybe it's because the younger generation of kids is just now catching on. I think that's what it is. I don't know how old you are, but St. Vitus was doing that shit in '87. It's been thirteen years. Who do they find out about St. Vitus from? From the Eyehategod guys? I think those guys are responsible for turning a lot of people on to St. Vitus because they'd always wear Vitus shirts, so there's kids coming up around that kind of vibe, like Eyehategod and Soylent Green. Eyehategod has been around for a long time. The guys in Corrosion of Conformity would have St. Vitus stickers on their guitars way back in the early days. Kids after awhile got tired of trash, maybe their minds are a bit more open to things that are heavier. I don't know. I'm not going to complain. It's just the way it is.

SST probably still has all the St. Vitus in print, but they are not in the stores, so kids have to go out and find them, perhaps on-line. But do you wish they might be re-packaged and somehow get back in the stores?

I would love to see them more available. I don't make a dime off any of that shit. Greg Ginn is running that show, so you can guarantee that it's going to be hard to get that shit. He's out of his fucking mind.

In what way?

He fucking mismanaged SST. He stabbed his friends in the back, like the Meat Puppets and Sonic Youth. He took them to court. He fought his friends in court. SST never fucking payed any royalties. Why do you think SST folded? Because instead of paying attention to Husker Du, Meat Puppets, and Sonic Youth, they fucking signed Run Westy Run and the Tar Babies and all that crazy shit. It's a classic situation. They'd be like, yeah we got five debuts this month. Yeah, that's great, but what about the fucking royalties?

When the Obsessed reformed, did you imagine it would be so short-lived?

When we got the Obsessed back together I really hoped it would be the real deal. We had no idea at all that we were in line to get signed. The guy from Columbia contacted us, but it ended up being a kind of nightmare at the time. But that's a whole other story.

They actually wanted you to re-record your music?

They wanted us to re-demo shit to be more radio-friendly. That's just not my way. I've never fucking sold out, and I never will. Of course, there's definitions of selling out, but I would never compromise my integrity to make some prick happy.

After the band broke up and you had a few years of substance abuse and overall bad times, you went back to Maryland.

I took a Greyhound bus.

What were thinking on the bus?

I had lost everything, so I was ready to start over, but at the same time I was still drinking.

That's when you took a couple years off from music?

I had actually taken a couple of years off before. When I got back to Maryland, I cleaned up my act up pretty quick. I partied a little while, but there were a few instances out here that made me realize, this is bullshit. So I quit drinking, and when I quit drinking I started getting strong again, and got all my will power back and quit everything. I never liked heroin, and that's my saving grace. Everybody I know that did heroin is dead or in jail. I was more into going up instead of going down. So I never developed a big heroin habit, I never had that problem. I took a real heavy trip and did some serious soul searching under a very heavy dose of natural psychedelics, which allowed me to phase out certain things that were blocking me, and that was good.

That was the point when you met the new era of bands like Clutch?

When we put the band together, we started getting out and playing shows with bands like Clutch.

Under a different name?

Yeah, we were called Shine, the same band, we just ran into a trademark problem with the name. Clutch took us out. They're a great band.

You knew exactly what you wanted?

At that point I was full-on into it. I was back into playing. I also knew that my music meant a lot to people, and my music meant a lot to me. So all the years I was down, those are lost years. It's all about the right people. You can't be happy playing in a band without the right people. When I met the guys, we kicked it around, and felt it worked real good, and it went from there. I never looked back. It was like a natural thing. It happened pretty fast, and it was good. We put a lot of fucking hard work into that band from the beginning. I mean, we rehearsed four or five nights a week every week.

And you met up with Joe Lally (Fugazi)?

Joe's a good friend of mine, even before Fugazi. He rented a room in my house back in the Obsessed days. He was an Obsessed fan, and really appreciated the stuff. He turned me on to Joy Division, and I turned him on to "Raw Power". We had that kind of relationship. And he was always a very responsible guy. I rented him a room in my house because I knew he'd pay rent. I was kind of intrigued, because he was a very cool painter. He was into Joy Division and stuff like that. He told me he wanted to play bass, and we talked about what he should get, and whatever, and it was all good. When I came back, he was like, this is cool, I would really like to put out a single. I got a label called Tolotta that puts out singles. Would you like to put something out? So we put out that single, and that's all he ever wanted to do, but it was so well-received, he thought, this is cool, maybe I can make it into a real label, then of course we recorded *Jug Fulla Sun* (2000). It's really interesting because our lives have intertwined in such a cool and unique way, all the way back when he didn't play, up through the time he's played in Fugazi. I saw him play the other night in front of 1,500-2,000 people outdoors at the park. He just wanted to do something to make people aware of my music in some way, so we did the first single. It was received well, and we said, this is cool. That's when he realized that this label thing was a serious thing. We have a great relationship. I have to tell you, my professional relationship with Joe is amazing because basically we made an agreement that if we ever needed lawyers, then we didn't want to do it. We don't have any contracts between us, but when he sends me a statement, he sends it on time. It's accurate, and I trust him 100 percent. Basically we have a 50/50 deal with him, which is unheard of. It's a works out great for everybody. We did a one off for Meteor City. That was all good, it was with Joe's permission. I thought that Chad was a really cool guy, I thought they were really on the forefront of the Stoner Rock thing when they released their first comp.

You had a cut on that?

Yeah, we had a cut on that. No, we didn't have a cut on that, we had a cut on the European one that followed. Anyway, I was impressed with Chad and what he was trying to do. He was breaking new ground and putting out these obscure bands that were really cool, like Lowrider, Fatso Jetson, that kind of thing. He was like, man, I really want to do something. I was like, what do you think Joe? And he was like, why don't you give them an EP, so I gave him the EP, and it did great, and then Chad decides he needs European distribution, so he wanted to go with Century Media, and everybody was like, no, no! Bad idea, look what happened to Eyehategod, bad idea. Don't do it. He ended up doing it anyways. It ended up being a totally bad deal for him. I just got my statement from him. We sold 1,500 records over there, and we made like 700 bucks or something like that. And now he's like, yeah, yeah, I'm trying to get out of the deal. But basically, it sucks. Here's what happened. We agreed to do this one off with him, and it was fine until they went to Europe, because Century is a terrible company to work with. We're getting paid these ridiculous low rates, and Chad got taken to the cleaners. And what happened to us? We got no advance, when he licensed Dreamwheel to them to manufacture, we got nothing, so they got a free fucking product. They're over their pressing the product with the fucking devil emblem on it and we're getting 50 cents a copy. It's totally fucking lame. One problem was I went along with Chad's licensing idea, even though I told him it was a bad idea. And it was a shady deal. That's the kind of shit I don't have to go through with Joe. I don't have to go through any of that crap with him. All that mumbo jumbo is gone. It doesn't exist.

You feel the kids are able to get the records?

Yeah, I'm just now starting to see people who are singing along.

So in fact, it's probably the best record deal you've ever had.

Well, I'm glad you feel that way. It's much better.

Spirit Caravan from Left of the Dial

Joe Lally and Wino

An Interview with Kim Coletta of Jawbox
Intro excerpted from Women in Punk

Throbbing bass player Kim Coletta shaped the equilibrium for Washington D.C.'s godfathers of angular, jazz-inflected, post-hardcore punk Jawbox, who always put integrity above profit while making albums that sound wide-open one minute and restrained the next. Like others of their ilk (Shudder to Think, etc.) they took the guardrails off punk and brought wholesale change to the genre, igniting a third wave of Dischord. Instead of anger coursing through their veins (like Minor Threat, SOA, Void) or harnessing openly left-wing leaning sympathies (Scream, Soulside), they chose an underlying sense of pure poetics while still remaining firmly in the humanitarian camp.

Whereas late era Government Issue (featuring Jawbox front man J. Robbins) yanked a few elements from the Damned and projected robust rock'n'roll back into the D.C. soundscape, Jawbox shifted gears towards more abstract and stylized sound structures that left listeners both enthralled and vexed. Between their well-honed, seminal albums *For Your Own Special Sweetheart* and *Jawbox*, Robbins charged ahead by writing lyrics that felt like Bob Dylan's leftover notes from *Tarantula*; in addition, with Coletta seemingly hyper-caffeinated behind her hard-driving bass, they paid endless homage to a cultural sea of influences, from Minutemen, Big Boys, and the Avengers to Frank Sinatra and Tori Amos.

Their power and majesty were evident from the first self-titled single forward, especially on tracks like the incessant, ready-steady-go "Tools and Chrome," which was re-cut to help anchor the first full-length Grippe. On the earlier works, featuring hard-pounder Adam Wade behind the drum kit, the band nurtured their post-Government Issue modern rock with punk gestalt, meaning the music is squarely within a more trad-rock camp ("Consolidation Prize," "Manatee Bound" "Grip") with strong hints of earnestness, flawless delivery, and conspicuous smartness. Coletta's bass playing thunders to the surface most prominently on tracks like the infectious, slightly low-key "Spit-Bite," the slower, tuneful, harmony-laced rev-up "Channel 3," and the lashing "Tracking," which administers dueling guitars with grinding efficiency and hardiness.

For Your Own Special Sweetheart inaugurated the era of drummer Zachary Barocas, which re-shuffled and rejuvenated the whole sonic imprint, one blistering track after another, starting with the barn burner "FF=66," in which Coletta's bass threads through the chaos like she is a soldier crisscrossing a minefield. The music is a basin of snapping drums, harrowing off-kilter guitars creating a lacework of noise, and honey-vocals turned sour shrieks. "Savory" became their modest "hit," flanked by Coletta's insistent stop-start bass, borderline ephemeral rhythm guitars, crunchy lead blasts, and the soothing cool vocals of Robbins. "'Breathe" sacrifices none of the fury, erupting like an evacuation notice, reclaiming all their punk heritage and allowing Coletta's bass to co-exist in power and triumph with the boys' hollers and twisting ribbons of distortion.

And when they do slow down (the expedition does not halt, though!) —from "Motorist" to "Cooling Card" - the tunes remain limber, bass-forward in the mix, potent, unfaltering and ever-coiling. Suddenly, out of nowhere, after some (in hindsight) slightly freshman-sophomore records, *For Your Own Special Sweetheart* became a billboard announcing the possibilities on the punk horizon, just as Mission of Burma had done. This album remains an opus of the era.

Kim Coletta by Chris Shary

Released just a few years later, their portent last, self-titled album features even more mind-bending, cornucopia drumming, from "Livid" onward to "Chinese Fork Tie" and "Won't Come Off," though they still remain capable of being surgically compact and able unleash distilled magma on "Mirrorful." The shepherded softer hues of "Iodine" also enrapture as the guitar lines helicopter to and fro. Yet, immediately the next blistering track "His Only Trade" is a helter skelter affair full of bass foraging and dual-vocal narratives that seem to weave, smack, and sneak into each other, which creates an agitated, harrowing sequence no Pepsodent can ease. However, like *New Picnic Time* by Pere Ubu (which seems like a distant relative to their *Modern Dance*), the tunes are challenging, inventive, and crack the walls of all predecessors, but also may be too - obtuse. The conventions of rock'n'roll shred into a million frays as they became nomads on some unknown musical expedition, which left some fans tilting their heads and raising an eyebrow.

Jawbox never tapped the dead buttons of redux, tried to create a Xerox of some long-gone cruder time, or commuted to the corporate world, even while making records for a major label. Along the way, Coletta also forged DeSoto Records, helping boost the path of admired bands like Compound Red, The Dismemberment Plan, and Beauty Pill.

And anyone who ever saw Jawbox live knows that she offered a ripe game on stage - a busy theater of thoroughly intoxicating energy at the fingertips of her sharp, unflinching movements. She never crouched like a helpless bird in shallow water. Lit by murky stage lamps, she struck out through her own secret routes in a music that launched a thousand post-hardcore fellow travelers, all eager to embed themselves in the contour of alt-music history.

I'm a bit devastated since Jawbox is playing Austin and Dallas, and not Houston.

I feel that when you go to Texas, and you only have a weekend, cause we're just conscribed by work and family in a way we weren't in our twenties, it was like you pick Austin, always, right? Like you just do that, then you pick Dallas or Houston, and that's above my pay grade, and I'm sure our booking agent had some reason for Dallas over Houston. I know we absolutely spoke to Houston promoters, and I couldn't say which has a better music scene. I have been so humbled to hear people, like in Boston, say "We drove 12 hours from Nova Scotia." I was like whoa, what the hell. It's been super cool. Some guy flew in from Salt Lake City to see us in D.C., and he requested that we play "Tracking," from *Novelty*, and told J. Normally, we don't take requests, right, I don't think any band does, otherwise it gets really crazy, but I made sure that "Tracking" was on the list, given how far this guy traveled!

I would make one simple suggestion: it would be incredible if you played "Sound on Sound" by Big Boys, an Austin band.

I was in touch with Tim Kerr, and I was like, if we learn this song will you friggin' come up and sing it with us? Tim did that thing, where he was like "Sure," but didn't commit. He's busy. I will tell you right now we did not learn "Sound on Sound," we decided to re-learn "Cornflake Girl" as a cover instead. Although, I suppose there is still time, but the will was there, and I even contacted Tim. I was like, "Are you coming to the show?" because that would be super fucking cool, but I think he is such a free spirit he has no idea if he is coming to the show. He could be in town, or he could not be in town. Who knows. Without him committing, I was like, hmmm...

Let's talk about your high school years. You've said you were an odd combo of nerdy/ jocky/new wavy. I know you are a big softball person, and you love baseball, does that mean you played sports in high school and listened to the Violent Femmes?

I did. I was on the varsity volleyball team and the varsity softball team throughout high school.

I always thought, because I was in sports too, there was a relationship between the skills you learn for sports and the skills you learn for music. Do you see it that way?

I have to think about that because I have always been terrible at learning foreign languages, and I always thought there should be a connection between learning foreign languages and music, but not for me, which makes me sad. What's funny is, I think we can take this in two different directions because a lot of people in the punk or indie music scenes were actively not sports players because they didn't like that vibe. Back in the day, it was a like a movie - the nerds, and the jocks, and the punk rockers. It was like really big cliques. I don't know if high schools are still quite like that. It seems, at least from what I have seen, a bit more blended. But I kind of moved between scenes. For me, there was no weird thing about doing sports and being in the punk rock scene. I had my people, but I would say my people were more punk rockers rather than jocks, even though I loved sports, and I still love sports.

So, I don't know if there is a connection. I do think, though, it may be as simple as hand-eye coordination, and things like that, is that what you are talking about? Maybe, but someone like J. Robbins from my band, he hated sports. I don't want to put words in his mouth. But that is still not his cup of tea. So, I dunno. It's a maybe on that. I'd like to think that there was a connection, in that there's something about the way you move. Then, my son is 18 now, and he can play any sport. He's just a natural athlete, and man, we could not get him interested in an instrument, and we tried forever. He loves music. But, boy, I remember when he was little, he turned to Bill and me and said, "You can get me piano lessons, but I am not going to practice!" We're like, "Why would we pay for that if you are not going to practice?" He's funny. He's done that School of Rock thing and enjoys learning like two notes on the guitar in order to play a Coldplay cover, or whatever, but besides that, there's no connection there for him.

You've said that you bolted with your friends from Nashua because that's the kind of people you were. What do you mean by that? Your not the type of people that want to feel stuck in a provincial town?

I wouldn't go so far as to call Nashua provincial, meaning it's the second largest city in New Hampshire now, and it was then as well. It's definitely different now. There was no diversity in Nashua. Yeah, provincial ... I am going to get myself into all kinds of trouble here! Fuck it, I feel that New Hampshire was a great place to grow up and felt safe, and was just okay. I actually remember, like it was yesterday, the first ethnic restaurant that came into town. It wasn't a Denny's, we had our first Mexican restaurant! It was like, "How exciting!" (laughs). Then we had Chinese and Mexican. It has changed quite a bit. It was just boring. Maybe provincial, but there wasn't anything to do! And maybe, I see this in my son because he lives in the Washington D.C. area, there's only so much you can do when you are a teenager. You are limited to shows that are all-ages.

I just feel we were restless and wanted bigger things, our group. We wanted to travel and see the world, and we felt constricted being in New Hampshire. We had wanderlust, which would be a better word.

Yet, it's where you saw GG Allin play gigs: was that a game-changer?

I did. Probably a game-changer in terms of what not to do, in terms of civility. I never found him inspirational in the sense of, "I'd love to carry my own feces around." No, but, super cool right? So outside the box in terms of anything I had seen. So, I feel it's a cool little thing I can say, "I saw GG Allin a few times in Manchester, New Hampshire." It was just weird. Probably not my cup of tea. I pretty rapidly got in and out of hardcore music because I really enjoyed melody. I really enjoy bands like Minutemen, Meat Puppets, and other bands that were pushing, Big Boys were another example, the boundaries of what hardcore could be, and being more melodic with it. I always leaned in that direction anyway instead of straight-up shouting men in hardcore bands. It's true, that's how I felt. I loved vocal melodies.

I loved that raw energy of the hardcore scene. The Boston hardcore scene was too macho (laughs) and male-dominated, but it was fun when I was a teenager. Looking back at it, it was cool to move to D.C. early on. There were a lot more women in the music scene in D.C. than Boston at the time, so, it was like, "Oh shit, it never dawned on me that I could do this" until I went to D.C., which I know seems crazy now, because so many women are playing, but it wasn't like that then. We would just sit there in high school and watch our male friends play in bands. I don't know why the light bulb did not go off sooner because my mom was a huge feminist in our town, which was highly unusual at the time. But I guess I was slow on the uptake, it took me to college to be like, "Wait, wait I don't have to just go to shows, I can try doing this myself." That was a super-cool moment in college when I realized "I'm going to try this."

But even D.C. seemed like a boy's club very early on in the hardcore era. But you were there for Revolution Summer, so did that open the door for bands like Fire Party and Autoclave?

I guess so, but it was different. Cynthia Connolly was in the music scene booking D.C. Space. There were just more women at shows I went to, which was refreshing. But yeah, Revolution Summer made a huge difference, and I was there then. I liked the D.C. music scene, but I wasn't constrained, I also loved what was happening, I said this in a recent interview, with Homestead Records and Touch and Go. I loved that vibe too. I wasn't just into the D.C. thing, but it was cool seeing bands like Fire Party. So being there made me feel like I could try it, but I was a good student, so I didn't try anything until after I got my degree. I knew not to push my parents in that way. I got my degree, and then we started Jawbox.

You've also said that you didn't learn anything practical at Georgetown, except for maybe about how to be an adult...

I am watching as my son is about to begin his own college journey. I think there are a lot of reasons to go to a university, and I think only some of them are academic, but I think it's a rare 17 to 18 year old who can say, "I am doing Nursing, I am going to study Nursing, I am going to be a Nurse for the rest of my life." It does occur, but I think it occurs less now than it used to in our society and I still think it's about becoming a global citizen and to learn adult stuff with training wheels. I think college is awesome, if you can afford to have that luxury. So, I am more practical. I am sure I would not be so draconian in my words now. I learned plenty of practical things (laughs). It's true, but that's okay. But in the classroom I learned to be a thinker and a writer, you know what I mean? I got a great Humanities degree at Georgetown, so thank you Georgetown. I think if I went back and could do it again, I think many adults would say this, I would do it better and differently, like "shoulda coulda woulda!"

In the time of Trump, I think a lot of people desire that era of widespread Humanities, since it builds an American identity that is different than a Trump supporter might envision.

Be more specific.

An immersion in the humanities suggests that we embrace a tolerant kind of democracy, so when we downgrade the Humanities, we get the kind of sectarian politics we have today.

Yeah, I would say that, and there's a drive today to do something more practical. Like, "Why would I major in history, what's that going to do for me economically?" But you're right. To do this at the expense of turning out people that are open-minded is bad, and I do think Georgetown was amazing at making me more open-minded. I happened to be the sort of person that was super left of center before going into Georgetown. The people I met were people like me, but also centrists, and people quite right of center, but people who were highly intelligent, okay? So, by lying on dorm floors until the wee hours of night and having that political discourse in a pretty civil way, it was pretty eye-opening for me. And it did inform me. Learning how to respectfully disagree with people is a cornerstone of democracy, but not any more. But, yeah, I am buying what you are selling.

It's funny because, listen, you are in Texas, so it's a little different, but on the East Coast and the West Coast, and I am grossly generalizing, but still, we're in a bit of a bubble. Like, even within my group of friends, we are very like-minded and I can most days pretend that things are smooth in our country because I go to dinner with people who are intelligent, civil, awesome, and clear-thinking, but I have been all over the United States, so I realize, that ain't how it is in lots of the middle of the U.S. Again, I am grossly generalizing here, but we need to get outside our little bubbles, or whatever those little bubbles are, and having Trump, and living in D.C. and experiencing the 4th of July, sometimes I do go to see the fireworks, but I couldn't deal with that bullshit happening downtown – between tanks rolling through D.C., his VIP speech, and ...ugh.

Politics now have unfortunately fallen into "I am in favor of whomever can beat Trump," which is almost a disappointing position for me to be in because I would love a multi-party system, so I could vote for someone who is really more radical than a Joe Biden or Elizabeth Warren. These people really don't reflect where I am coming from either, but oh well. If either of them is going to be the best bet, then I am all in, but it's like a compromise. "We gotta beat Trump" is where my head is right now.

With tours right now, including your own and Soulside in Europe, people just don't long for the music; they long for punk's past – the protests at the South African Embassy, the free concerts at Fort Reno Park, when bands seemed really active, socially committed, and on the streets, and I'm not sure we are seeing that in the same way anymore.

I don't think so, but Fort Reno continues, and benefit shows continue here in D.C. It's maybe not the same level of engagement. So, we're using this tour to do a bit of outreach and activism, like we put together this super-cool thoughtful flyer that took some time on our part to describe these causes that we support. So, we encourage fans to pick up the flyer and really think about it. Now, at a Jawbox concert, there's mostly like-minded people, although (laughs) some friends were telling me a story recently about when J. said something from the stage that was anti-Trump in D.C. the other night, some guy rolled his eyes. Whatever, there's always gonna be a few Jawbox fans that are Trump supporters (sighs). But when our activism is limited to a flyer, I dunno, maybe we could play a benefit show, and I have been to marches, I have, not as many as I did in my twenties because life is interfering, my busy adult life. I don't know if that is just an excuse or not. I think about these things a lot. I agree with you. Although there are lots of people doing similar things, though they may not be in our music scene. That's okay.

Let's talk about your label DeSoto. There seems to be a secret history of women in punk that gets overlooked: the women behind the scenes, like labels, from Frontier Records to Simple Machines.

I just saw Kristin from Simple Machines, it was really cool to see her again.

Do you think there needs to be a book or long article that addresses that part?

That's interesting. I don't know if it would make a book, but at least an article, Women behind the scenes. To me, the next frontier, and I will get back to your question and get the train back on the track, I think ... Well, I'm on tour, and I have not toured in a long time, and we're playing purposefully with bands with women in them, and that is awesome, and would I like to see more racial diversity, and other kinds of diversity in our music scene, sure, but I cannot exactly control these things. But I look at the tech people at the clubs, and they are still mostly men. The kind of house people, all the sound engineers, and monitor people, except when I went to Brooklyn Steel in New York recently and there were women doing sound stuff. I thought to myself, yes, this is the next frontier, like women in more technical positions. To me, it's all like, whether doing a zine or a label or sound, I think it's powerful to have women because they are so under-represented. It would make for a cool article, actually.

I bring it up because you have described how early on you encountered sexism on those same levels - like the sound guy who jokingly asked if you knew how to plug in your bass.

The #metoo movement made me go back in my mind and bulldoze through my mind and look at things through a new lens, and think, "Yeah. That sucked." It's funny because Tierney Tough, from the Pauses, from Orlando, FL, were playing shows with us, and she had a recent incident with a sound guy at a club down south. It could have happened anywhere, but it happened down south. And I'm like, "This bullshit is still happening!?" It's not my story to tell, although she did share it with me the other night in D.C.

I wish I could go back and do some of my interactions with these men differently. I would have been bolder and louder and clearer in purpose, but it's intimidating, and I was young, and there weren't many women around. And often these things happen as one-to-one things, like there weren't other people around to support me or help me. And we talked about this, Tierney and I, we talked about the moment when you are like, Oh, what do I do because I have to work with this person the rest of the fucking night at the club, and they can literally sabotage me in different ways. She actually confronted this person, but at the end of the night. Not that I was voiceless, but my default position then, it sure isn't now and hasn't been for the last 10-15 years, would just be to blow it off and move on and say, "What a fucking asshole." My position now would be, "Let's have a discussion here about what you just said." I have not been encountering that type of thing at the clubs we have been playing right now on this tour: they are awesome people, professional, so I don't expect to encounter anything like that. We'll see. You never know.

You're a media tech at a library?

I've had many hats at the school I have worked at over the years. The last two years I have been both a librarian and doing academic technology. But next year I am moving, again, into 6th grade English. I've done 8th grade English and 6th grade History, I have been a Latin teacher, I've had all sorts of roles.

You're a 'jack of all academic trades'!

Yeah, jack of all trades, master of none (laughs). I like re-inventing myself every three to five years. I like adapting to new roles.

But that speaks to the importance of the Humanities, for it allows you to do that.

It does, and I feel that I can teach any grade, really. I love big picture thinking, although I have been working with younger kids, who definitely bring a different kind of energy to the room. I am used to middle school students, but I have been working with grades 3-5. And I'm at an all boys school, so I have a lot of male energy around me. That's okay, I really like it! I have a son, I work with boys, I work with men in a band, so it's not like this is some new situation. I have lots of female friends to get me through the male energy.

Speaking of libraries, how do you feel about the D.C. Public Library and University of Maryland archiving D.C. punk history – do you worry about punk being institutionalized as flyers and record label material go into such places?

I've actually work with John Davis, who's from Q And Not U, a D.C. band, and he's a librarian archivist at the Univ. of Maryland, and I know the people that work at the D.C. public library archives. In fact, the woman who heads that up, her dad is also a teacher at the school where I work. D.C. is like .6 degrees of separation. It's a pretty small city in the scheme of U.S. cities. We're no Houston, this is much smaller, and we kind of know each other in various ways. As a librarian, and actually I am trained as an archivist, that's actually my Master's Degree, so I think it's cool. I don't feel it's weird because the people doing it have all the right intentions, which is preservation of information. And there's so much fucking information out there bombarding us all the time that if we don't curate it, it will be lost. To me, it's that simple. So, I don't have any problems with it. I don't think it is selling out to the University of Maryland, some sort of scam. I'm good with it. That's a good question. It's a unique question.

Your son just turned 18 – what's harder, being a mother or being in a band?

Oh god, being a mother. It is so much harder. Being in a band can be hard. I must say that this go-around with Jawbox is much better in the sense that we're all grown ass adults now. So, I think we are informed by things that happened, like over the past 20 years, and we can treat each other with, even when we disagree, respect. 20 year olds don't have those tools in their tool belt yet! Like, we had a really democratic songwriting process in Jawbox, which would lead to all kinds of angst. But I think it's what made our songs good, that sense of putting them through the ringer like that, but it took a toll at times, for sure. There are lots of hard things about being in a band, but parenthood is like ... do you have kids?

No, I do not.

It's fucking messy. They are like giant X-factors. You know, people make those jokes all the time, there's no handbook, although lord knows people have tried to write books about parenting, but every kid is so unique. They can have a good minute, and then a shitty minute. My son is really stubborn, smart, and funny. And the highs can be really high and the lows really low. So, it's like a roller coaster. Yeah, I found it harder. I think the X-factor explains it best! From day to day, year to year, they are constantly changing, and there's pro and cons in every stage of child development. Some people lean more towards the younger kids, while others like older kids, but I look at him, and I look back at how they can't wipe their own ass, that sucks, but they are so cute, then the next year they are toilet trained but then acting out in this way. Now I'm just watching him enter adulthood, like he tells me a lot that "I'm eighteen now blah blah blah," and he'll demand something. And I'm like, "You're so not a grown adult." You know that as a parent, but they think they know everything and that they're invincible. The teenage years are sort of scary. Like, okay, you put them behind the wheel of a car, let's say. And you know they are dumb-asses. Sure, your kid is always amazing, polite, and driving the car carefully, but they are still dumb-asses. It's like a wing and a prayer, the teenage years, when you go into adulthood. When I look back at my 20-year-old self, or whatever, when I was hanging out with my band-mates or friends, you just always think you know more than you actually do (laughs). But you can't tell a kid that. They don't want to listen to that. I get it.

One of my favorite moments with you recently is watching you share social media of you practicing Jawbox songs at home on your stereo: you seemed to have so much joy as you played it. When you had to re-learn the songs, what was the most surprising thing to you?

The most surprising thing was that sometimes there was muscle memory, and sometimes there was not. Some songs I could re-learn in ten minutes, others took me three weeks to re-learn. I am not talking as if I spent three hours a day on one song, because I would get burned out, but it was like, okay, "I've got a few more bars of whatever song under my belt, so I am going to move on to other things now." So, I wrote out bass tabs as I re-learned all these songs, so I'd never have to go through this again (laughs). I have a whole collection of bass tabs for all the songs we play now. I don't mind admitting that sometimes I re-learned the songs because others had learned the song and posted the bass tabs on-line! I would go on-line and be like, "Yeah, here it is." That was funny too because sometimes they were right, and sometimes they were not-so-right. I was like, "Ah, honey that's not really..." But it was a jumping off point. There are not bass tabs for all the Jawbox songs on-line, unless I did it, and I know I will never get around to that. It took longer than I thought. I think we learned over 30 songs. We have a few more to learn, like "Capillary Life." It took a year to prepare for this tour, and we practiced a lot this year. We knew if we wanted to do it we wanted to do it right.

Do you find the songs as gratifying as when you wrote them?

I think it's more gratifying. I think J. and Bill are singing better than they sang when they were younger. It's more deliberate; it's more intellectual. J. has done this cool thing - he has taken vocal lessons this last year and now knows how to warm up his voice before a concert and cool it down. Bill has taken on those exercises as well. I think we are more thoughtfully listening to each other. It was unbridled in our twenties and thirties. We look at each other in the eye now and play better. It's just fucking cool. I think the energy is still there. That's what people have told me. I am going to have to believe them.

JAWBOX EDSEL
ALL AGES
$7
FRIDAY FEBRUARY 24
DOORS 8 PM • TICKETMASTER
THE EDGE
100 WEST LIVINGSTON DOWNTOWN ORLANDO

the JESUS LIZARD TAR JAWBOX craw
TUE SEP 1ST
PEABODY'S DOWN UNDER
1059 OLD RIVER RD.
CLEVELAND FLATS, OHIO 44113
ALL AGES
DOORS 8pm
$10adv.
TICKETS AVAILABLE AT: All TicketMasters

From Los Angeles
On Texas Hotel Records
Ex-Black Flag
HENRY ROLLINS BAND
From D.C.
Ex-Government Issue
JAWBOX
With Chicago's Own
Snake Eye Recording Artists
BHANG REVIVAL
DOORS OPEN 6:00
SHOWTIME 6:30
TICKETS AVAILABLE AT ALL TICKETMASTERS
ALL AGES
THURSDAY MAR. 22
EXIT 1653 N. WELLS

FROM OUR NATIONS MURDER CAPITAL, WASHINGTON D.C.
JAWBOX
ALSO PHILE 13 WHAT'S PROVEN?! AND KARL
ONLY $5.00
IN FORT COLLINS
APRIL 12 AT THE GRANGE
FRONT RANGE RECORDS
COFFEE CORE PRODUCTIONS
STARTS AT 7:00

SHEER STABB

An interview with the former front-man of Government Issue. PART ONE

Like always, *Complete History* is a bit misleading, since the second volume does not have "Dali's Sunflower" (the Shonen Knife cover), "Forever" from the *Odd Man Out* compilation single, or the entire EP on Giant that had different, self-mocking versions of "I'm James Dean" and "Teenager in a Box" and several live cuts. Could you explain what governed the decision to leave off these tracks? Was it simply licensing, or other issues? And don't tell me it's because of space, because the CD has double live versions of "Jaded Eyes" and "Mad at Myself," among others.

The *Strange Wine* EP, and tracks from *Beyond* like "Forever" (originally on *Odd Man Out* EP) and "Dali's Sunflower" (originally on *Every Band Has a Shonen Knife Who Loves Them*), were left off for a couple of reasons. First, we were primarily interested in putting out a version of *Finale* which had previously been available only as an especially hard-to-find live bootleg on the German label Lost and Found. The double-LP did eat up a lot of space on our Volume II and squeezed our options for additional bits and pieces. Second, we chose not to include *Beyond* on this volume because Ian Mackaye wants to feature his version of "Asshole" from that collection on Dischord's upcoming anniversary box set. We thought it would be special for Dischord to use that track now without competition from a simultaneous *Beyond* re-release. Whether we ever put it out again is up in the air.

We've discussed matters with Dr. Strange and have decided to re-release *Strange Wine*, but this time we'll include our entire CBGB performance instead of just the seven live tracks that made it onto the original album. Tom and I are extremely excited about this and think it will sound amazing. In its entirety, the show wouldn't have fit on Complete History Vol. II. Just a side note—also, Counterclockwise records in Belgium are re-releasing a lot of G.I.'s original vinyl such as *Make an Effort* and *Boycott Stabb*. Tom and I have been incredibly pleased in our relationships with both Dr. Strange and Counterclockwise.

During the *You* and *Crash* period, Government Issue and Naked Raygun were doing a cover song of each other, which later happened with Helmet and Jawbox, and now again with NOFX

and Rancid. In Naked Raygun's case, they released a live version of "Where You Live" when they re-released their records a few years ago. What Naked Raygun song did G.I. perform, and was it by accident, or who was responding to whom?

Unfortunately, I think some of your facts are a tad off. Naked Raygun were our friends, but we never covered any of their songs. Both groups had nothing but admiration for each other's work and felt like musical brothers. We eventually played a show together—I'm pretty sure it was at WUST Radio Hall in DC—and everyone had a great time. It meant a lot to us when they told us that our *You* album was the best record of '87! They particularly dug "Where You Live," so in tribute to Raygun, we started adding "Whoahhs" to that song on a few of our final shows. That's as close as we came to covering them. Don't get me wrong; J. and I (both huge Raygun fans) would've loved to cover one of their songs, but we knew we could never do them justice. Most of all I could never sing like Jeff Pezatti. Only last year, I finally checked out *Last of the Demohicans* and discovered that Raygun had covered "Where You Live." That was the most flattering thing a band has ever done towards G.I., and their version is brilliant!

Government Issue did few covers. "These Boots are Made for Walking" by Nancy Sinatra and "Trapped" by Faith come to mind, but did you know of 7 Seconds' hardcore remake of "These Boots..." when you recorded it? And how did you end up doing a half-time version of the Faith song?

You mean G.I. didn't do "Boots" first? If 7 Seconds did theirs before '84, then they win the "who can cover Nancy Sinatta first" contest. It wasn't till years later that we heard about their cover. The funny thing about our version was that all the NYC skins really took to it like their anthem: These boots are made for moshing! I loved the song as a campy, biting reaction to a lover's betrayal, but a lot of folks made it into this bad-ass tribute to their toughness.

As for "Trapped" by Faith, Tom and I loved that band and wanted to cover that song. It took a lot of hemming and hawing from the ex-band members before they let us do it, but they finally caved when we promised to treat it with the respect it deserved. We slowed it down, that was Tom's idea, and added a little metal flavor for the

"I'LL GO ON RECORD AS SAYING THAT EVEN NOW, I THINK I'M ABOUT 70% PERFORMER AND 30% SINGER."

studio version. But we only played the song a few times onstage before deciding to shelve it. We didn't think it gelled. I love Marc Alberstadt's drumming on the studio version, though. He lifted the drum roll from Ozzy's "Crazy Train," and to me, that's the best part of our cover. Of course, many punks thought we had gone metal at that time, but it was always fun confusing our audience.

You mentioned earlier that you liked Naked Raygun better than Big Black. I remember giving Shawn from Swiz my copy of Atomizer when they toured with Soulside, but I would never have given away my Naked Raygun records. "I'll always prefer Naked Raygun doing Big Black's 'Peacemaker' than Big Black doing Big Black," you've said. Why?
J. was the first person I knew who really dug the Chicago punk stuff. He turned me on to Raygun, Effigies and Big Black. I was never really into the Effigies, liked some of the Big Black songs from *Atomizer*, *Songs About Fucking*, and their version of Cheap Trick's "He's a Whore," but I loved the Naked Raygun. A song like "Peacemaker" owes a lot to Big Black, but I guess I just prefer Jeff's vocals over Steve Albini's. Also, Raygun never got into the drum machine thing like Albini loved to work with. I dig that Big Black have a strong Killing Joke influence, but I'm just not a big fan.

Brian Baker said that while Government Issue was a good punk band, Dag Nasty kind of defined a generation of hardcore where a band could play slower, a singer could really sing, and it could still be considered punk. But what seems odd about the statement is that it relates to Government Issue's self-titled LP just as much. Would you agree?
That's a mighty bold statement for anyone to make. Nothing against Dag Nasty, but they certainly didn't "define a generation" of anything. Neither did G.I. Some folks like the Dags, and some like G.I. And, scary as it may sound, there are some who actually like both bands. I do think that Dag Nasty were an impressive band at certain moments in the eighties. But G.I. had proved all that playing-slower, singer-that-could-sing, punk nonsense Brian's talking about by the time we

did *You*. Our self-titled album accomplished some of that, but I can't say too much about my singing on that one. I mostly talk-shouted-sang at that point. I really wasn't too confident about my voice until *You*. And I'll go on record as saying that even now, I think I'm about 70 percent performer and 30 percent singer. As for Dag Nasty, I think Dave Smalley did some fine work on *Can I Say* and sang up a storm live; but, honestly, I prefer his stuff with All and Down By Law over Dag any day. Dag's first release just came off as a continuation of Minor Threat for me. I don't think they truly came into their own until *Field Day*. Peter Cortner's debut on *Wig Out at Denko's* was part of their Descendents-influenced thing, moving to California really changed their sound. Peter's vocals and the musicianship on songs like "Things That Make No Sense," "All-Ages Show," and "Trouble Is" are commanding and edgy, really original. Those are three of the most well-crafted pop-punk songs ever written. Even so, I dig Peter and Colin Sears (after they parted briefly from Dag) on their Los Vampiros album *Less Than a Feeling* a lot more than their work with the Dag Nasty. I think their version of Abba's "Mama Mia" is brilliant.

[Brian] also mentioned that one of the reasons that Dag Nasty has fared well over the years is because their records were on Dischord, which has kept them in print, whereas until recently Government Issue records went in and out of print, perhaps ending up outside of listeners' radar. Was one of the driving reasons behind releasing the Complete History discographies to look back and wink or to reintroduce the band?
Well, he's right about that. The Dischord name sells like hotcakes. And there are still people out there who think we had some fallout with Dischord and had to move on. The truth is that Tom and I would've loved to stay with Dischord in '82, but the timing just didn't work out. Ian and Jeff Nelson really needed to release *Out Of Step* because Minor Threat were heading on tour. That was at the same time that G.I. was getting *Boycott Stabb* ready. Dischord couldn't fund two releases at once, so we just looked for an alternate label. Ian and Jeff generously let G.I. have *Boycott Stabb* come out as a split release as Fountain of Youth/Dischord. And Ian did a wonderful producing job on the record. He definitely got the best version of "Sheer Terror" out

of us. After that, Dischord had other bands to get out, so we ended up fending for ourselves. Tom and I went through a lot of hassle with our next weasel label which isn't worth naming, but is worth shooting, during and after the band's existence. You wouldn't believe how much crap they gave us when we tried to gain control over our back catalog. A couple of years ago, Dr. Strange records came to us with the proposition of re-releasing our early stuff as *Complete History Volumes I and II*, and we went for it. We are extremely happy with how that's turned out, even though our former weasel label put up a big fight over our later material and delayed Volume II by about a year. In letting us have complete control over the artwork and liner notes, Dr. Strange has been the most honest label (apart from Dischord) that we've ever had the pleasure to work with. They're some of the nicest folks Tom and I have ever dealt with, as well. We weren't trying to prove anything to anyone by putting out the *Complete Histories*, nor were we aiming to re-introduce the band. It's just nice that everyone who ever truly cared about G.I. has the opportunity to check out all this stuff the way it should've been released in the first place. And tacking on some things like the hard-to-find *Finale* and a few never-released live tracks is just a way to give the people who appreciated what we did a little something extra. The funny thing is that most people cannot believe that we really never made any money when we existed. It's not like either Tom or I make boatloads of cash from these re-releases, but Dr. Strange has treated us with respect and some decent royalties. So, it took us twenty years after the fact to finally make a profit. I once wrote a letter to *Big Takeover* fanzine about their mentioning G.I. in their list of all-time top 100 punk bands. I said, "I wanted to put my two cents in, because that's about all we ever made back in Government Issue!" And the really pathetic thing is that's no joke.

When I met you years ago on tour in Madison, WI you were still working as a bike messenger (if I remember correctly) when you were not on the road. You mentioned that if things didn't blossom for the band, you would have to basically give it up. Did you really think, as your liner notes suggest, that you could have become the next Replacements or Hüsker Dü whisking around college campuses and only bad management was holding you back?
At that time, I was a foot courier and both J. and Pete were bike couriers. And oh yeah, Tom was a car courier. We all had a silly day job between tours, but instead of making money in G.I., we kept

losing it. Being in a punk band in the eighties was a money-losing proposition. It would've been nice to play the same circuit as Replacements or Hüsker Dü, and I did believe it could happen. But there were about a billion reasons besides bad management holding us back. It was only in the last few months that we were able to get a booking agency to manage us because, for years, everyone dismissed G.I. as just this little hardcore band from DC without a marketable future. Even with this new management, though, our former label, who deserve to be tortured very slowly… (like J. used to say, "As you can see, I'm filled with nothing but love"), wanted us to eat shit for one more year with the hope of phasing out our radical following and steering us toward the college-campus circuit. Their strategy was to get us more mainstream acceptance and bolster our chances to get signed to a major label. But our struggles toward solvency weren't going to get any better: We were supposed to agree to do little out-of-town mini-tours strictly for the recognition. I wasn't about to ask my employer for a couple of days off only to lose money. In fact, in doing these types of shows, we'd have put ourselves further in debt. No freaking thank you. We definitely wanted to escape being in a hardcore rut and to avoid the possibility of running into neo-Nazis at our gigs. But I was starting to feel my heart wasn't in it any more. Things were rough for us on that last tour. Tom and I were both frustrated enough to contemplate breaking up the group. Our tempers were always raging, we took it out on each other, and it just wasn't worth the battle any longer. People still think G.I. should've stuck it out one more year, but they weren't in our shoes. Tom and I are friends now, but we're lucky we didn't kill each other back in the group. I have no regrets about G.I. ending when we did. All the younger bands already thought of us as dinosaurs, but I'm glad we didn't become a bunch of tired, posturing geezers just going through the motions. There are plenty of punk rock reunion bands to fill that void. I'd like to think that we quit while we still believed in the music.

Plus, you saw the terrible, late-version, post-Chris Mars Replacements and were mightily disappointed. How far would you have gone to be like that?
Man, don't remind me. I think the Replacements circa *Let It Be*, *Tim*, *Pleased To Meet Me* are brilliant. But they truly should've hung up their attitudes after Mars blew that pop-stand! Seeing one of the finest songwriters on the planet, Paul Westerberg, and an excellent guitarist

"I'M GLAD WE DIDN'T BECOME A BUNCH OF TIRED, POSTURING GEEZERS JUST GOING THROUGH THE MOTIONS."

"VERY FEW OF THESE NEWER GROUPS HAVE REALLY PAID THEIR DUES. THEY WILL TRULY NEVER KNOW WHAT IT'S LIKE TO BE IN A PUNK BAND."

songwriters on the planet, Paul Westerberg, and an excellent guitarist like Tommy Stinson trying to reenact their drunken antics (when they were sober!) by spitting on one another onstage was one of the saddest things I've ever witnessed in my life. And that hack studio drummer they played with was so beneath their talents. He sure wasn't Chris Mars! I saw a bad attempt of some guys trying to be the Replacements and went home bummed. If G.I. had ever begun to head towards that pathetic territory, I'd have walked off stage and never looked back. Luckily, Pete, J. and Tom never got drunk or spat on me during a set. I'd probably have killed one of them if they had.

Why was Government Issue's luck almost as bad as Black Flag's luck?
Well, I think Flag's got G.I. beat when it comes to being burned on the road. But we did endure our own chunk of that shit back in the eighties. For some of us, it was just the wrong timing to be in an underground punk band. G.I. managed our band badly. Some of the other punk bands of that period actually had better business sense and/or management to make sure they weren't getting ripped off. Down the line, G.I. had contracts with our promoters; but even so, sometimes a contract amounted to a laugh in the face from the people paying you at the end of the night. Many of our "guarantees" weren't honored. Whenever some weasel club owner screwed us over in one town, we just moved on to the next gig in hopes of making up for that loss ... provided that the weasel gave us enough for gas. We dreaded any days off because, as a struggling band, we needed the money. These days, groups connected with punk haven't had to suffer the way bands like us or Black Flag did. A lot of us old punks paved the way for these new kids. But I do think there is a need to really struggle for a while just to earn your way into the music biz. Very few of these newer groups have really paid their dues. They will truly never know what it's like to be in a punk band. When bands like G.I., Minor Threat, or Flag started, we were thankful to have a few gigs that didn't even pay anything because we just wanted to play and get our names out there. We didn't start to get paid even a handful of dollars until a year or more after our first show. And, like Flag, any money we made at gigs was put back into the band immediately. Granted, unlike Flag, we never lived in a rented office space or slept in cardboard boxes. That's the real hardcore life! But they chose to do that. And we all knew the deal: None of us expected to get rich from this underground music scene. Although being able to pay the rent or, at the very least, the light bill, would've been nice. I'm not envious of these

new kids getting their huge-money, major-label contracts, staying in luxurious hotels on tour (instead of crashing on someone's floor or the van), purchasing a mansion with all their expensive toys and ending up on "MTV Cribs." That's just not my scene. Ian said it best a few years ago when asked about bands like Green Day and the Offspring: "These bands are the Ugly Kid Joe's of the nineties: They will soon be forgotten." The same can be said in 2002. Some music is timeless and others are simply pointless.

You stressed the importance of the Damned's *Strawberries* and *Black Album* back in the late-1980s, and still do, but they play very few songs off of those records while on tour. Is the Damned suffering from some kind of punk revisionism, and why do those albums define the greatness of the Damned to you?
The Damned were so good during the eighties that it's tough to think about them today. Their stuff with *Machine Gun Etiquette*, *The Black Album*, and (my favorite) *Strawberries* are classic. They obviously influenced many who came on their heels, like TSOL. Currently, bands like the Offspring owe practically their careers to the Damned and TSOL. Government Issue owe the Damned a lot, too. If it hadn't been for, say, *Strawberries*, our S/T and *You* albums wouldn't be the impressive recordings they are. Captain Sensible hugely influenced both Tom Lyle's and Brian Baker's guitar sounds back then. And I'd be an out-and-out liar if I didn't admit how much Dave Vanian influenced my vocals on those G.I. records. Unlike their last few, the Damned's new album *Grave Disorder* isn't completely horrible in terms of songwriting. But its best moments are lifted from their past. The Captain and Vanian have a few good songs together, but even the best cuts are like third-rate *Strawberries* or *Black Album* tunes. As for their touring without Rat Scabies (the most savage drummer since Keith Moon!) in this new line-up, I can't buy into it. I saw the Damned play only once, on their *Phantasmagoria* tour (not a bad album, actually). Sensible wasn't with them, but Vanian and Scabies worked so well together that it was a fun show. I would've killed to see them during their *Strawberries* tour. Sadly, the current tour looks more like a bloody "Punk Rocky Horror Picture Show" than anything cool. But as far as The Damned playing "very few songs" from their past, I've seen recent playlists online that report they've played songs from *Machine Gun Etiquette* all the way to *Strawberries* mixed in between their new stuff. Of course, they want to push their current material because they beat the old songs into the ground for a hundred years. I understand that from the

for "Sheer Terror" or "Notch to My Crotch" when we wanted to play our newer ideas instead. G.I. rarely asked our audience, "Okay, what do you want to hear?" I'm not down with the concept of playing requests before an audience. If the Damned really don't include too much from their early catalog, I don't think it has anything to do with "punk revisionism"; they're just trying to explore fresh musical territory. But, the old grey Damned ain't what she used to be. Still, if Dave and Sensible are making some money after all the years they put into that band, then more power to them. They both deserve their due. I guess that's why they're trying to give it another go and finally make a living of some kind with this new album deal and tour. For me, it's a little too much of a nostalgia gig. I think they should've moved on about seven years ago.

Could you please describe who/what Giant Records really was? Most people might see the label as a kind of Slash records that built up bands like Dag Nasty, Verbal Assault, and Government Issue just before collapsing and almost erasing those same bands from the face of the earth. The liner notes from Vol. I say that they printed vinyl and cassette versions of *Boycott Stabb*, but did that happen in 1983, or did they re-issue it when they re-issued the self-titled record too?

Well, you are referring to Giant (bunch of bloodsucking weasels) Records, right? They were a label formed out of Dutch East Trading Company, which is a distributor. Alas, G.I. was their first naive victim. Other punk bands, like Dag Nasty and Marginal Man and Verbal Assault, were on the label, but I don't know if they received the same ass-crap treatment that we did. I'm pretty sure that Giant reissued *Boycott* on vinyl and cassette when they reissued *S/T*, but I'm not positive. Since they weren't paying us anyway, why keep track? All the people who go out and buy our old albums on Giant/Dutch East India will be paid a dime. According to our lawyer, as of several years ago, they legally owed Tom and me each at least a couple thousand dollars, Mark, Pete, and all the revolving bass players a little less. That doesn't even account for reprints they've sold before and since, for which they hoodwinked us into signing away any royalties. But we've gone through enough lawsuit-threatening drama with them, and they finally don't own our material anymore. The sad thing about all this is that they were an indie label who screwed us like a major would've done. I think everyone who's been cheated by Dutch East, from us to Sonic Youth, would like to stand in line and take a shot at the staff. Sometimes, you can really get shafted by an indie label, too. So beware, kids.

For ten years, it seems that no one spoke of Government Issue, then suddenly Kerosene 454 covered "Man in a Trap," Hurl covered "Understand," and the two Dr. Strange volumes have arrived. What do you think has drawn young people back to the band?

Who really has the answer to that one? It seems to me that there are two big reasons that could make sense. First, there's a new breed of young punks who have discovered G.I. from their older brothers' or other relatives' collections. I know this one very eager and confident twelve-year-old who writes me online, whose "cool uncle" turned him on to G.I. It's amazing that this kid will quote me my own lyrics or stage patter and knows all about my past just from interviews in old 'zines. So, you have this audience of young folks who weren't even born when G.I. was around, and the closest they can come to being right there at one of our crazy concerts is listening to the albums. Second, these bands that are covering our songs might see Government Issue as a band that created really honest music, and they just want to show their appreciation for what we did. I never wrote dishonestly when it came to my heart, and the rest of G.I. always crafted our songs with a powerful, emotional edge. The songs some of these bands have chosen to do are emotionally pretty deep. It doesn't seem that anyone's covering a silly song like "Rock and Roll Bullshit." They're picking ones like, say, "Where You Live," "Understand," or "Teenager in a Box," which were all pretty gut-wrenching for me to write. And the bottom line is that good songwriting is timeless. Kerosene's version of "Man in a Trap" is quite good, but I've never heard Hurl's take on "Understand." Outcrowd do "Understand," too, on the *Punk Rock Jukebox Volume I* compilation. Also, Kustomized's version of "Bored to Death" (with Peter Prescott of Mission of Burma and David Barbe of Sugar) and Stomach's takes on "Mad at Myself" and "World Caved In" are quite impressive. And a couple of newer bands, Casket Lottery and Hot Water Music, have released versions of "For Ever" and "Jaded Eyes," respectively, on a split EP. I haven't gotten hold of that yet, but I'm looking for it. A young local DC band, Brace, recently told me they cover "Plain to See" during their shows, and they want me to come up and join them to sing it sometime. There's even a Finnish band out there, Valse Triste, who sing "Teenager in a Box" as "Paastakaa Ilmat Pois." That's a trip. Maybe one day, someone will gather up the many G.I. covers for a tribute album? Who knows? It's the highest form of praise to have someone cover your song. It's really cool that there's a loyal audience out there who cares about what my old band did. I enjoy meeting and talking with people who say G.I. meant a lot to them then and now. I've noticed that some other fellow musicians dismiss their punk past, but I'm proud of what G.I. accomplished and will never dismiss it. I'm happy to talk with folks about the G.I. days and hope that some of them will actually buy my book of memoirs, *The Evolution of Sheer Terror*, when it's finally published. But I also hope that these same people who appreciate my past can listen honestly to what I'm doing now in The Factory Incident. Some might not dig it, others might enjoy the group. All I ask is for folks to give us a chance. So far, a lot of old fans of G.I. have responded really positively to The Factory Incident. That's very cool.

To be continued...

BOYCOTT DEATH

A TRIBUTE TO JOHN STABB

Government Issue singer John Schroeder (aka Stabb) refused to play the punk rock game. Known to wear lengthy tube socks or groovy 1970's thriftstore ware, he taunted audiences by being the epitome of uncool. His sardonic vocals and quick wit thrived alongside the bracing guitar compiled effortlessly by wall-of-sound Tom Lyle. Sadly, Stabb died after a harrowing bout of stomach cancer.

At their hardcore peak, 1982-84, Government Issue were an incisive, breathless, zealous act whose songs eviscerated annoyingly happy people, uptight fashionites, religious rip-offs, and useless new wavers. Stabb wove these subjects into lightning-fast songs, thereby defining hardcore as a humorous alternative to mere jock-anthems for buzzed hair crews. By the time the album *You* debuted in 1987, the band had morphed into a fine-tuned, rhythmically muscular, melodic rock'n'roll unit with an underpinning of psychedelia and a punk inner core. And his post-GI bands, like Factory Incident, explored nuanced, smart modern rock that highlighted slight British shoe gaze tendencies as well as other artful leanings, not unlike Morrissey's *You Are the Quarry* period.

In the late 1980s, Government Issue stayed at my parents' house in the Illinois/Wisconsin stateline a few nights after playing Madison, where the venue (lined with immaculate wooden floorboards) made the gig-goers and band peel off ragged boots and weathered tennis shoes, as if enacting a dizzying punk sock hop. Years later, I interviewed Stabb for my zine Left of the Dial. The piece stretched over two issues (No. 4-5). Both Stabb and I bonded over shared interests: we both loved *Strawberries*, an overlooked morsel by the Damned, and Randy "Biscuit" Turner of the Big Boys. Plus, Stabb really was a gossip column and could dish some dirt, surprising me with his onslaughts (that will remain unpublished).

"See ya in the punk tabloids!" he signed off in an email to me in 2002. And that's how I will recall him - tongue-in-cheek, a wise guy, but a singer of unusual prowess and emotional depth too. Goodbye Stabb.

SHEER STABB

An interview with the former front-man of Government Issue. PART TWO

When talking about Factory Incident, you've recently said, "I haven't felt that kind of closeness to band members in years, and it feels great." Do you mean literally (there was a long hiatus between Glee Club and Factory Incident), or do you mean to suggest that the band has a chemistry together that might have been missing with your earlier bands?

As far as the chemistry goes, yes F.I. is far different than G.I. in the fact that we all hang out with one another when we're not playing together.

There's something that brought Karl Hill and I together the same way all of us were drawn to each other: his love for my voice, a common goal musically, cool ass people, etc. Our chemistry on stage is important when everything is working perfectly and we really get our ideas across. Or even our writing together... it just clicks.

I think our "common goal musically," is to do something different, and open-ended – to challenge ourselves and work with

different people. And just see what happens? Just like Glee Club, it's cool trying out new ideas and collaborating with new people is something that I've always done – there wasn't this "long hiatus" – and F.I. is just the latest step in that whole process/philosophy. Though we may have started out with a more specific sound in mind, it was too limiting to a bunch of people who love a tons of music, from punk noise to melodic pop noise. Perhaps for practical matters some bands narrow their focus out of necessity and work toward a more genre-specific sound or they'd never produce squat – it's a huge challenge and slow process.

So maybe our musical chemistry isn't instantaneous (From the fantastically whacked-out sound of my post-G.I. group, Weatherhead, everybody in that group didn't listen to the same records!), but it's ultimately more rewarding when it comes together, as with a live performance.

In G.I., you usually "cut loose over a distorted guitar," though on songs off the *Crash* record there was some crooning. If you looked a bit towards Dave Vanian in late period G.I., what kind of models, if any, do you approach as F.I.'s singer to capture the perfect "dreamy post-punk band" sound?

I've used the word "crooning" as a joke – I'm certainly not singing like Perry Como or Sinatra (Nancy or Frank). So let's just say I sung more melodically on *Crash*, and with The Factory Incident, I'm just trying to challenge my voice more. For my vocals, I really just get to use that emotional (and if anyone uses that idiotic term "Emo" to me, I will be forced to kill you!) thing.

Our first recording and its mood (I added atmosphere) but Karl said we're going into a more edgy direction and that's perfect –

if that can be elaborated on it might be cool. It's all added up for F.I. The mood when we were writing those songs, the mood in the studio, the darkness of the recording, because of how we were all feeling at the time we wrote the songs. Karl thinks I'm one of the few exceptions in this rock music genre that has a completely unique voice.

Factory Incident

"THERE'S A PRETTY BROAD SPECTRUM BETWEEN SCREAMING AND CROONING AND BETWEEN SKRONK AND MELODY THAT WE WANT TO BE FREE TO EXPLORE."

We're going to do our full-length soon and reiterate the direction we're going in: moody and atmospheric still...though more edgy and angular.

There's a pretty broad spectrum between screaming and crooning (that's called, uh, singing?) and between skronk and melody that we want to be free to explore, along with whatever mood it suggests. Similarly, what we listen to — individually and collectively — is across the board and constantly expanding, so any part of it that inspires any one of us may work its way into our songs in some mutated way. That may be a vague and generic statement (the ol' "we don't wanna be pigeonholed" dodge) — but it's really more about how we want to create and keep evolving. That of course includes building upon what we've learned from recording the songs, which captured a certain mood that was representative of that period in time but didn't convey as well the power we've become more aware of from performing live and from practicing and writing since then.

It sounds like F.I. is in for the long haul. You've suggested that even other band commitments or living in different places won't stop the momentum- "we'd still continue- during vacations or sending music electronically." Yet, would those constraints begin to re-shape the sound of the band? Shared electronic files sounds like F.I. could become a cut and paste project reminiscent of Unkle or Moby.

What we meant is that if we were ever in that position we'd find some way to work on ideas separately and/or in small groups — we'll never, ever have anything to do with electronic music. The concept of this group as we've developed over time is to leave it open-ended. If we were to go on hiatus and circumstances arose where we couldn't get together the way we do now we'd try and revisit the project from time

to time and see what happens. It's a good creative outlet and the majority of us should keep it going. Moby? Unkle? I dug Moby's video with the hot babes Christina Ricci and Fairuza Balk in it, but nobody in this group listens to that crap! And I grew up watching *The Man From Uncle* but I guess it's not the same thing. I despise techno, rave or flaccid house in any shape or form!

It's just a logistical, practical thing — exchanging sound clips or song ideas on tape, CD, MP3, whatever — to keep communication and the whole process going when we're not in the same room. Obviously, the collaboration itself would be pulled together in the most organic way possible or it'd be boring as shit.

Why has Factory Incident decided to go the DIY route and not wait for a label to pick the CD single? Was it just the tradition of who you are and where you came from, or the simple advantages of total control? I assume your name is a selling point.

The basis of any band is to write music, record the efforts, release the music in some fashion and perform the music live so naturally we just went with that "DIY" or whatever you want to call it mentality. Screw, "Do It Yourself"... for us it's more about just doing it. Whether you pay for the recordings out of your own pocket or you have some label pay for it shouldn't be an initial concern.

But now, it's time to move on. Julian Cope had a great quote about people who want you to stay in the past. The interviewer asked Cope "Would you ever go back to do Teardrop Explodes again?" Julian's response was "Would you ever want your mother to wipe your ass again?" I love that one. Brilliant.

UNK THE CAPITAL

BUILDING A SOUND MOVEMENT

THE RISE OF PUNK AND HARDCORE IN WASHINGTON D.C. 1976-1983

LM SCREENING!

special guests
DENVER!
:lan Theater
urs.Oct.17,7:30pm-$9

Bad Brains
Minor Threat
Slickee Boys

Q & A with filmmaker
James June Schneider

@punkthecapital
vww.dcpunkrockdoc.info

Punk the Capital! Chronicling the History Of D.C. Punk!

An interview with filmmakers Paul Bishow and James Schneider
Previously published on my blog The Center for Punk Arts, Nov. 2014

What do you think are some of the great misconceptions of DC punk?

JS/PB: One of the things we cover in the film is the whole scene that preceded the Bad Brains in D.C. in the late 70s, that small but fairly cohesive group of people working together to build something. I'm not sure it can be called a misconception but definitely the pre-1980 DC punks deserve a lot more attention, historically speaking. The other thing is the Straight Edge movement. Drugs and alcohol just weren't what the younger punks were looking for. The excitement and the establishment's reaction to the music was enough. So the whole "boredom" thing just didn't enter into the equation. The energy of the music and all the things going on around the scene made for constant activity. Drugs and alcohol just didn't have a part in that new and intense DIY ethic. That was part of what harDCore was about beyond DC as well.

Does this documentary try to flesh out details or elements that books like Dance of Days could not, or did not?

JS/PB: First of all, Dance of Days was a major accomplishment in covering such a large time frame of DC punk, including the later DC punk period of the 80s and 90s that often gets less attention. Our film elaborates on the generational and cultural shift happening in DC circa 1979. We dive back into what happened before then, in the late 70s, and then after, with harDCore. We get to the heart of why DC Punk has such staying power, why harDCore had to happen, and why DC was such a fertile ground for this new scene. The answer to these questions come straight out of that transitional moment, and specifically the Madams Organ artists co-op. It's something you can pick up on when all the pieces are assembled and when you see all the interconnections between the generations and how they perceived each other.

Looking back into DC punk origins, do you think bands like Slickee Boys, Tru Fax and the Insaniacs, and White Boy were just as vital as veteran punk bands in NYC, like J/Wayne County, Dictators, etc?

JS/PB: Definitely on a local level they were. These were bands you might see a couple times a month and that saw each other even more. They were as important in DC as those NYC bands you mentioned were to NYC. And DC has a tradition of hard working bands, whatever kind of music it is. Those early bands knew what was going on and had their antennas out. Those DC bands you mention were a huge influence on the younger generation, if not musically, at least in terms of proposing a model of how non-competitive and community-like a music scene should be. In our film, we also go into how they also showed the younger generation the basics of DIY.

Much of DC punk has often been associated with Dischord, yet Pussy Galore, Half Japanese, and Peach of Immortality also sprouted. Why do you think harDCore gained such a strong presence in history and lore compared to other scenes?

PB: For me, I loved a lot of the non Dischord bands like Half Japanese or the Velvet Monkeys, but also remember, not all Dischord bands sound or sounded alike so I wouldn't say there was just a "Dischord sound" either. Dischord definitely had a huge presence, to the point where bands even setting themselves up as anti-Dischord such as No Trend. But really that is just the dialectic of punk, all in good fun... DC harDCore took hold and spread widely largely because of Dischord's well-organized sense of mission, they really did want to change music from bottom to top.

I know the film has taken ten years: did any painful truths become evident - personas, unmasked, limitations understood, places and people lost forever?

JS: Several people we interviewed have passed away since we started this film and several DC Punk landmarks have been transformed into condos or Starbucks. So there have been some major changes in D.C.'s character but that really has helped us in how to think about D.C.'s identity in our film. So our doc has hugely benefited from the time it's taken, including a lot of technical advances that will help with all the archival work. Also, some people are more willing to talk more than they did before, some less, but I would say overall that folks are now taking stronger positions and thinking more about about that history.

Some proceeds will benefit Positive Force, an iconic force within the conscience and outreach of DC punk. Do you think it helped re-ignite the ethos of local punk right as many critics saw it waning in mid-late 1980s?

PB: I do not think the conscience of punk waned.

JS: It definitely was part of the politicizing of DC punk, which was not a bad thing. I grew up going to those early Positive Force shows so my early exposure to any kind of political consciousness came from those events and the bands that were singing about issues. Then I could go see other local bands or out of town bands and get a totally different flavor, there were choices. It's worth pointing out that even before Positive Force DC began, harDCore was on the outs and a lot of people in that scene were looking for a new direction, Positive Force became part of that evolution.

I know that punk in DC should be spoken in the present tense -- bands still emerge. What ones today, do you feel, link to the spirit evident as in the mid-1970s?

JS/PB : There's a resurgence of a harDCore scene happening in DC these days which is cool, but the links with the older scene are not always what they could be. That might be changing. In the meantime, the younger scene calls that 1980's generation the "olds."

Apart from the fan rituals (zines...) and band performances, what part of the DC punk legacy still deserves much attention -- perhaps art and photography, like Jeff Nelson, Cynthia Connolly, and others?

PB: I think mainly what we know now is that the influence continues (though not always recognized) in terms of the directness of the ideas and presentation. The art of thinking for yourself. That's the very basic ingredient of Do-It-Yourself.

JS: In terms of Dischord, there's an esthetic that has aged well, and those people you mention were a big part of that and hold a sizeable place in our film. But I think it's important to point out that this whole younger generation thought that something important was happening, which is why there were so many people documenting it. They were right.

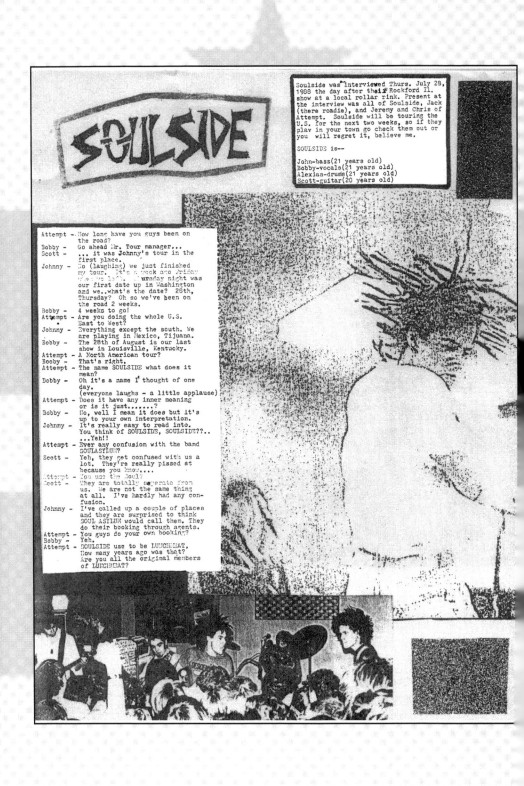

SOULSIDE

Soulside was interviewed Thurs. July 28,
1988 the day after their Rockford Il.
show at a local rollar rink. Present at
the interview was all of Soulside, Jack
(there roadie), and Jeremy and Chris of
Attempt. Soulside will be touring the
U.S. for the next two weeks, so if they
play in your town go check them out or
you will regret it, believe me.

SOULSIDE is--

John-bass(21 years old)
Bobby-vocals(21 years old)
Alexias-drums(21 years old)
Scott-guitar(20 years old)

Attempt - How long have you guys been on
          the road?
Bobby -   Go ahead Mr. Tour manager...
Scott -   ...it was Johnny's tour in the
          first place.
Johnny - No (laughing) we just finished
          my tour. It's a week ago Friday
          we got back. Thursday night was
          our first date up in Washington
          and we..what's the date? 26th,
          Thursday? Oh so we've been on
          the road 2 weeks.
Bobby -   4 weeks to go!
Attempt - Are you doing the whole U.S.
          East to West?
Johnny - Everything except the south. We
          are playing in Mexico, Tijuana.
Bobby -   The 28th of August is our last
          show in Louisville, Kentucky.
Attempt - A North American tour?
Booby -   That's right.
Attempt - The name SOULSIDE what does it
          mean?
Bobby -   Oh it's a name I thought of one
          day.
          (everyone laughs - a little applause)
Attempt - Does it have any inner meaning
          or is it just.......?
Bobby -   No, well I mean it does but it's
          up to your own interpretation.
Johnny - It's really easy to read into.
          You think of SOULSIDE, SOULSIDE??..
          ...Yeh!!
Attempt - Ever any confusion with the band
          SOULASYLUM?
Scott -   Yeh, they get confused with us a
          lot. They're really pissed at
          because you know...
Attempt - You use the Soul?
Scott -   They are totally seperate from
          us. We are not the same thing
          at all. I've hardly had any con-
          fusion.
Johnny - I've called up a couple of places
          and they are surprised to think
          SOUL ASYLUM would call them. They
          do their booking through agents.
Attempt - You guys do your own booking?
Bobby -   Yeh.
Attempt - SOULSIDE use to be LUNCHMEAT,
          How many years ago was that?
          Are you all the original members
          of LUNCHMEAT?

Bobby - Johnny isn't.
Johnny - I decided not to join the band.
Bobby - Actually what happened was -
let's see.. LUNCHMEAT was 84'
85' and then we all went to school.
We came back for the summer of 86'.
Bobby - and got SOULSIDE together with
the exact same members of LUNCHMEAT,
and then after that summer re-
corded an album.
Attempt- Into different music too?
Bobby - Yeh.
Scott - We didn't want to play the old
LUNCHMEAT stuff.
Attempt- What's the difference between the
LUNCHMEAT sound and SOULSIDE sound?
Bobby - Soundwise I would just say SOUL-
SIDE is a little bit more advanced.
I mean after your first year at
college you do throw up a lot.
Scott - We take SOULSIDE a lot more seri-
ously than LUNCHMEAT, with LUNCH-
MEAT we were just having fun. When
we got SOULSIDE together we wanted
more of a serious band. You know
let's really think about what we
are doing.
Attempt- How long was SOULSIDE together before you recorded the first album?
Scott - We recorded the first album in the
summer of '86, but it didn't come
out till the summer of '87.
Johnny - It was on SAMMICH/DISCORD Records.
Attempt- When is the new album going to
be released and are there any
changes music wise compared to the
first album?
Bobby - I think the biggest change between the two albums is lyricly,
the lyrics and ideas on the new album are a lot more politically aware,
we're more involved in what's going on in the sense I mean the
first album was not more (as HRR put
it) personally political.
Attempt- So the lyrics on the first album
were more personal ideas?

Bobby - Exactly, I mean the lyrics are
still personal, but we're in-
vovled with the thing - politics
on a personal level. I still write
personal lyrics. I happen to be
a vegetarian now and that's personal to me.
Attempt- Who in the band is vegetarian?
Bobby - Half of us. Johnny and I are.
Johnny - Musically also the new record seems
to be a shift away from the traditional hardcore sound for at.
Scott - It's groovy.
Bobby - It gets more into a groove.
Scott - Instead of like..CLICK CLICK CLICK
2 minutes musically grind, everybody going off, it's like drums and
bass will be grooving for a while
then I'll bring the guitar in, then
the vocals coming in as much more
of a sparce type minimalistic sound.
Attempt- Any stories about what happened on
the road this tour?
Johnny - Last September when we toured the
country we stopped by Jimmy Swagart
Ministry. We didn't get to play,
but we ran around naked.
Scott - I've never been Baptised so I wanted
to Baptise my entire body.
(laughter)
Bobby - Not to many crazy things have happened to us.
Scott - We've never been robbed!
Johnny - Bobby was sort of robbed. Wasn't
it while we were waiting for a show?
Bobby - Oh yeh that's true, I got robbed in
Boston. My wallet was stolen.
Attempt- Who writes the songs?
Scott - Usually the way it works is I
might play a few guitar riffs then
Johnny and me and Alexias get together and put the music down and
then we start jaming on something.
Bobby fits vocals to it and we get a
grove together and we all throw ideas
in and next thing you know we have a
song!
Johnny - Sometimes Alexias gets a beat and we
put music to that.
Scott - Those are the kinds of songs that
turn out groovy because we write it
all on the same wave lengths. I do
not like coming up with the song on
my own.

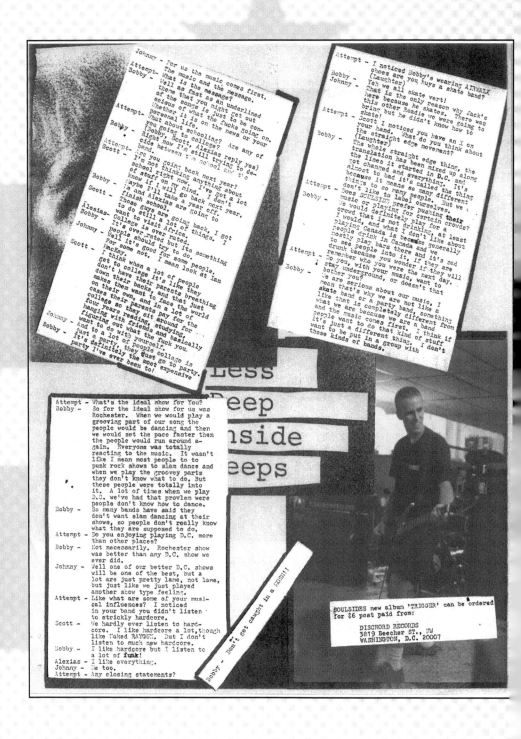

Johnny - For us the music comes first. The music and the message.

Attempt - What is the message?

Bobby - Well as fast as an underlined show that you just get out of the songs is just to be conscious of what the fucks going on. Whether it is on the news or your personal life.

Attempt - What about schooling? Are any of you going to college?
(Bobby, Scott, Alexias reply yes)
Right now I'm still trying to decide between the school and the band.

Scott - Are you going back next year?
I'm not thinking anything about school right now. I've got a lot of stuff on my mind. Maybe if I will...

Bobby - Me and Alexias are going to finish school.

Scott - Those guys are going back, I got to do still a lot of things. I want to visit Africa.

Alexias - College is over rated. It's over rated but its something people should try to do.

Bobby - Well it's good for some people.

Johnny - For some not. I mean look at Ian Mackay.

Scott - I think when a lot of people get to college it's like they don't have their parents breathing down their backs and that just makes them want to face the world on their own, and in a lot of cases their parents pay for the college so they sit around for four years reading, studying, hanging out with friends and basically figuring out what the fuck you want to do with yourself.

Johnny - And to a lot of people college is just a party, they just go to party.

Bobby - It's definitely the most expensive party I've ever been to!

Attempt - I noticed Bobby's wearing AIRWALK shoes are you guys a skate band?
(Laughter)

Johnny - Yeh we all skate vert!
That is the only reason why Jack's here because he skates. There was this other Roadie we were going to bring but he didn't know how to skate!

Attempt - Scott I noticed you have an X on your hand. What do you think about the straight edge movement?
(Laughter)

Bobby - The whole straight edge thing, the translation has been mixed up along the lines it started in D.C. and got changed and everything. It's almost to bad it's called the thing because it means so many different things to so many people.

Attempt - Does SOULSIDE prefer pushing their music or playing for certain crowds?

Bobby - We would definitely play for a crowd that is not drinking, at least I would, and what I don't like about playing Canada is because people drink in Canada and generally mostly play bars there and we to see people into it, if they are drunk because you wonder if they will remember who you were the next day.

Attempt - Do you, with your music, want to stay underground, or doesn't that bother you?

Bobby - We are serious about our music, I mean that's why we are not like a skate band or a party band, something like that is completely different from what we are because we are a band and the music comes first. I think if people want to do that kind of stuff it's just a different thing, I don't want to be put in a group with those kinds of bands.

Less
Deep
Inside
Keeps

Attempt - What's the ideal show for You?

Bobby - So for the ideal show for us was Rochester. When we would play a grooving part of our song the people would be dancing and then we would set the pace faster then the people would run around again. Everyone was totally reacting to the music. It wasn't like I mean most people to to punk rock shows to slam dance and when we play the groovey parts they don't know what to do. But these people were totally into it. A lot of times when we play D.C. we've had that provlem that people don't know how to dance.

Bobby - So many bands have said they don't want slam dancing at their shows, so people don't really know what they are supposed to do.

Attempt - Do you enjoying playing D.C. more than other places?

Bobby - Not necessarily. Rochester show was better than any D.C. show we ever did.

Johnny - Well one of our better D.C. shows will be one of the best, but a lot are just pretty lame, not lame, but just like we just played another show type feeling.

Attempt - Like what are some of your musical influences? I noticed in your band you didn't listen to strickly hardcore.

Scott - We hardly ever listen to hardcore. I like hardcore a lot, though like Naked RAYGUN. But I don't listen to much new hardcore.

Bobby - I like hardcore but I listen to a lot of **funk**!

Alexias - I like everything.

Johnny - Me too.

Attempt - Any closing statements?

Bobby - Don't get caught in a MOSH!!

SOULSIDES new album 'TRIGGER' can be ordered for $6 post paid from:

DISCHORD RECORDS
3819 Beecher ST., NW
WASHINGTON, D.C. 20007

US- You just released your first record, and on your own label. Why did you choose not to go the route of Dischord, Sammich or some other established D.C. company since most of the people that helped on the production of your record are from those two labels?

KF- There are a lot of reasons why we decided to release the record ourselves, none of which have anything to do with our personal relationships with Dischord or Sammich crews. We relied on both for advice and support, but in the end decided that if we put it out ourselves, we'd have the flexibility we needed to respond to whatever situations arose. For instance, we ended up giving away a couple hundred to college radio stations, a thing that neither of those labels do. We also used it instead of a demo when dealing with promoters. Had we done it through one of the labels, we couldn't have done either of those things. Also, KING FACE doesn't really sound like most of the bands that are on Dischord or Sammich. It would be misleading to those who bought the record because of its label and would hurt us in the long run.

US- Do you plan to release other records on this label?...Just yours or other bands?

KF- No way. We're sick of doing it.

US- You've been around for awhile yet it seems that not that much has been heard from you. Do you play out much?

KF- As often as we can. We've been taking it slowly, letting things build of their own accord, pushing it only reasonably and letting it grow. Also we had a lot of personnel changes around the beginning, so that was an impediment to getting to more people sooner.

US- What took you so long to release some vinyl?

KF- Why force it? When the time was right, we jumped. Playing has always been our first priority, anyway.

US- Your lyrics seem to show that you pretty much focus on real feelings (topics whatever) You seem to feel strongly about what you write. Who has influenced you lyrically? Why?

KF- Impossible to say. In my writing, as well as in our music, if something is obviously influenced by something else we tend to avoid it. We like to stress instead group effort and originality, though rock and roll is a somewhat limited universe.

US- Who has influenced you musically? Why?

KF- Again, who knows? Everything we've ever heard, anything we've ever formed an opinion about, either positive or negative. We all come from diverse backgrounds and it all gets recreated in the mix.

US- I've heard that the singer from Soul Side is Mark's younger brother and that your bass player Andy Rapport is related to Adam Rapport. Is any of this true?

KF- Both of those statements are true. Interestingly, both sets of brothers are twins.

US- Mark, you've been into the D.C. music scene for a long time. Since your days with Ian and Jeff in the Slinkies, you have probably seen a lot of bands come and go (in D.C.). What do you think of some of the younger D.C. bands?... Do the members hold as much promise as all you guys did?

KF- First of all, none of us old scenesters held any promise. We did it the way we felt like doing it and took a lot of shit for being talentless idiots. As for the younger bands around (some of which have some very old members) there are a lot of good ones and a lot of shitty ones. We pay no mind to see the ones we like and are content to leave it to others to judge their relative past or future importance.

US- Will D.C. remain as crucial as it has been for the last seven years?

KF- I have no idea. Once upon a time I would have said something to the effect of, "Yes, because we dedicated members of the scene will never let the heartbeat of the city slow and will never sell out or get old or lose energy..." but that of course would have been wishful thinking. I don't really think about the scene anymore, though I know that there are those who do. I just go to shows occasionally and play when we can.

US- Do you associate or play with many other D.C. bands, such as those on Sammich or like Fire Party or are you more off on your own?

KF- A little of both. I love to play with a lot of the bands from around here, especially ones with whom we're friends, Fugazi, Fire Party, Soul-Side, Scream, but out of town it's tougher because we're not stylistically compatible with a lot of them. It can make for disappointing shows.

US- Does everyone in the band stand behind the lyrics or is it more like each person has their own instruments. And the words are just Mark's instrument for personal expression.

KF- Our lyrics aren't a position. I write them, but they're nothing to stand on or behind. I would hope that the other guys in the band at least like them.

US- Mark, some of your lyrics seem to be written while you're going through something and some seem like they're written after the fact, after you've gotten things figured out. Do you think it's easier or better or anything to write about things while they're happening, or is there a better perspective while you're looking back, kind of out of the

Interview and Design by Tad Keyes

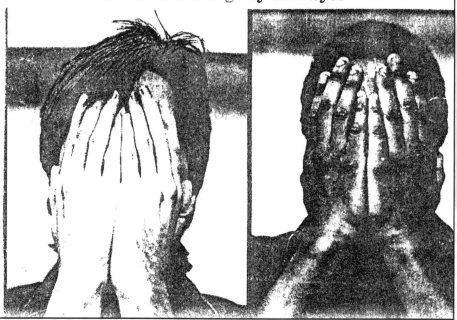

out of the situation?

KF- Life is a balance between passion and perspective.

US- What does the name mean?

KF- Everyone acts differently around different people. Different faces for different situations. KING FACE is the one you wear when you're alone.

US- Any touring planned?

KF- When the time is right, which looks like any day now.

KING FACE
2706 North 4th St.,
Arlington, VA. 22201

lick the moon
just another one i used to know. why talk when there's nothing to say. friend, I lay my baggage by the road side and I walk away. the past is like a closing door, there's nothing here for me no more. why save when there's always more? my eagerness betrays me, plenty of this and none of that. seems like I've spent my whole life trying to lick the moon.

crawl into tomorrow
my eyes are closed, but I feel the moon. sleep confuses now with soon. I want to open my head, I want to let in the night. I want to howl at the moon, I want to bathe in its light. daytime takes me unawares. I smash my head through the veil of the night and crawl into tomorrow. I want to go. I want to chew the truth of "I don't know". I want to look at a word and not have to read. I want to grip the flame inside of me. daytime...

THIS INTERVIEW WAS CONDUCTED THROUGH THE MAIL, BY ME, IN JANUARY THANKS TO MARK FOR BEING KIND ENOUGH TO ANSWER IT

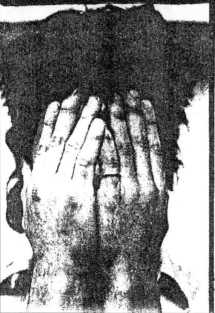

The Make-Up at Emos, Sat. Oct. 3rd, Austin.

Rising from the tumult of their weekly Chocolate City (Washington D.C.) gospel hour, the Make-Up came to Austin in a full-tilt resurgence of bastardized funk-soul-punk. Having recorded their last studio record with the help of Royal Trux, the quartet gleamed the most frenetic cuts and threw in a couple of old singles, including "Blue is Beautiful," an ode to pills and a newly defined American mod culture.

Donning solid black outfits that resembled a collision between Mao Tse Tung , the Secret Service, and an episode of *Lost in Space*, the group threw themselves at the brink of disaster as Ian, their priest and irreverent front man, climbed the sweaty, skinny shoulders of the young throng that pressed against the stage. Several times he attempted to vault across their heads, aiming to reach further and deeper into the bobbing expanse, but was futilely kept at bay by the rickety unstable leanings of the crowd. Never to be out done, he continuously grasped overhead beams, pulled himself above everyone, microphone engulfed in his mouth, and screeched his blood curdling Marvin Gaye-on-helium routine. The new songs, including "Black Wire Pt. 1," "Live at the Rythmn Hive," and "Earth Worm Pt. 1" were knee-deep exorcisms of the soul, and kept up the pace, generating a hubbub of dancing bodies and "Yeahs" from the crowd.

According to recent interviews in *The Hedonist* and other mags, the Make-Up is still about animating a real rock n roll "dialectic," a role that requires constant musical upgrades. Their sound began as a loosely regulated combat Gospel punk, replete with preacher antics and synchronized, ping ponging grooves, all framed within their "sound verite" experimentation- no effects, no bourgeois overdubs, no technological hassle. The result, almost always flattened and tinty, felt like a ride in a rock n roll dingy. Now, they've beefed up their sound, incorporated an even more trenchant Marxist perspective on their plight in the music business, and edged their music to the shoreline of 1970's blaxploitation musak, and keyboard work that resembles Stereolab.

As an extra pleasure, Kid Congo, formerly of the Cramps and the Gun Club, played the triangle, tambourine, and belted out some backup vocals. Although he's probably 15 years older than the band, he still felt like a right buttock to their hip swagger. And as Ian proclaimed, "Oh baby, there's a lot of mosquitoes out there. A lot of vampires, but we gotta make it happen. Gotta get beyond the fences out there baby," then set loose a sharp intake of maximum noise, the crowd giant-stepped away from Emos and into a holy space where only the Make-Up have the key.   -David Ensminger

The Oblivion Kid's pelvis arched up, genitals flapping as he

pirouetted across the crammed space alongside amplifiers perspiring. With a compulsion that rioted in his bones, his neck undulated, and his muscles flexed in a berserk swoon. The movement, the physical act, seemed to unlock his code of inhibition, drawing him to the other side of libido, where the inner and outer geographies broke down. His body writhed furiously, agitated and epileptic. The word-speech "Testify" clambered through the microphone pores. And soon, hooked to the tail spinning Chocolate City groove which befell the aural zones of the record store, The Oblivion Kid's feet switched from larval to cantankerous (and back) with every note, nearly swinging his callused toes out of his retread Sear's boots as the Gospel crooned hard and chaotic. Mouth cottony with phlegm, bits piled in the corners, teeth bared in the verve and clamour of things, he slackened for a brief time, then flung himself into the Osmosis Waltz, or the Lumpen Jig..."Destination Love" like a razor to his old habits and frequencies (lack-love, politics, complacency and other forms of rigor mortis).

He danced, danced, danced, eyes wide as frying pans, numb from cigarettes and bad breath. On the breaks which hung like the shadow of a steel and glass high-rise (the interludes of heartbreak alley or a collapsing light wave) he poised himself on the brink of tumult, then flanked by kinesis (gasoline explosion kick drums, bass crescendo), with the guitars producing goosebumpin-pricks along his forearms, he jettisoned his old-modes for the unbrokered Gospel.

Gospel of no-slack groove...Gospel of cancelled Time...Gospel of long and disintegrating rhythm...Gospel both primer and helix of human imperfection...Gospel from the lungs of Daedelus...Gospel from the church of nothing...Gospel of the next five minutes...Gospel squeezed into his back pocket...Gospel which breaks the ribs of the new Lusitania...Gospel de-funked and inverted...

Gospel, which, routed from the causalities of pop decor (the famished trump card of disco), in which each line, each cue, each dictum was flawlessly spewed...The Gospel, which, lifted high, jumped nerve-naked, (un)legislated in a halo of patent-leather and gleaming oil...Gospel which was a precise and ineluctable vaccine in the festering pile of Squaredom, burning towards Memphis and Peoria, towards the periphery of these states, towards the glands of boy/girls in the trachea of night.

PHOTO BY GLEN E FRIEDMAN

BLACK GRAIN1/GOS:EL YEN-YEN PRODUCTIONS
DISCHORD RECORD COMPANY,WASHINGTON,D.C.

The Make-Up by Chris Shary

FUGAZI

COMING TO NEW BRUNSWICK FOR A REASON.

60% OF N.J.'S HOMELESS ARE CHILDREN.

SEPT 25 8PM

ALSO PLAYING: CHICKEN SCRATCH & THE BOUNCING SOULS. RUTGERS STUDENT CENTER - MULTIPURPOSE ROOM. SPONSORED BY R.U. WITH THE HOMELESS TO BENIFIT - MIDDLESEX INTERFAITH PARTNERS W/ THE HOMELESS. INFO 249-1364. $5.00

VERBAL ASSAULT

FUGAZI

SOUL SIDE

RAIN CROW

$5 AT THE WILSON CENTER ON DECEMBER 29, 1988

a positive force d.c. benefit for the homeless

HOW ABOUT A FROSTY

HOUSE SPECIAL: PINNOCHIO'S

FUGAZI!?

FUGAZI WILL APPEAR WITH

MARGINAL MAN
IGNITION
FIRE PARTY

4 COURSES - ALL YOU CAN EAT

COME WITH A SMILE

7:30 PM
ON THE 3RD OF SEPTEMBER (A THURSDAY)

AT THE WILSON CENTER
15th & IRVING ST. NW
5 DOLLARS TO BENEFIT POSITIVE FORCE COMPILATION RECORD

THE RETURN of the ORIGINAL

SCREAM

Beefeater (Beefeater)
+ DOVE

SATURDAY AUGUST 24th   8:00 PM
WUST RADIO MUSIC HALL   9th & V St. NW

ADVANCED TICKETS AVAILABLE AT:
Penguin Feather Records (Georgetown, Rockville, Bailey's Crossroads, Vienna); Commander Salamander, Joe's Record Paradise Too (Wheaton); Yesterday & Today Records (Rockville)

TICKETS $7.50 ADVANCED $8.50 AT DOOR

* Plus Special Guest

SOUL SIDE
first 1P still hot

IGNITION
anGer meAns new 7" out + 1st one   now!

1P	sea	air		7"	sea	air
$5.	$6.	$10.	SAMMICH RECORDS PO BOX 32292 WASH DC 20007	$2.5	$3.5	$5.

BEEFEATER
& RITES OF SPRING
& GREY MATTER

and you'll never hear surfmusic again

toMAS

AT:
OOD FOR THOUGHT
conn. ave.

number of dollars: 5

on to the warpath.

time: 10:00 PM SAT Sept 20

Skeeter Thompson and Amy Pickering by David Ensminger

By Burt Queiroz

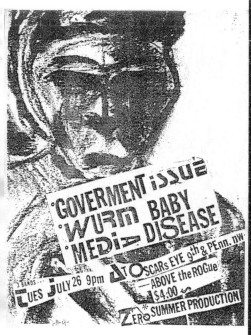

GOVERMENT ISSUE
WURM BABY
MEDIA DISEASE

3 BANDS TUES JULY 26 9pm

OSCARS EYE 9th & PEnn. nw
— ABOVE the ROGue
$4.00
ZERO SUMMER PRODUCTION

GOVERNMENT ISSUE
TRUE SOUNDS OF LIBERTY
MARGINAL MAN

Fri. Nov 9
Wilson Center

8 pm $5

AAAAGGGHHHH!
ITS "SCREAM" WITH

King Face   SHAVED PIGS...

NO ALCOHOL

AT THE ANTHRAX
SAT. DEC. 19th
25 PERRY AVE,
OFF. RT. 7. NORWALK. CT.
R.B.R.

Presents   Don't miss this great show!!!

DIRECT FROM D.C.

SCREAM
AND a RETURNING! FROM RENO!!!
maybe
7 SECONDS
—WITH—
JACK SHIT

AND WITH SPECIAL GUESTS

RZM

SUNDAY
AUG 14
SHOW
AT 8:30

DON'T MISS
THESE 4
GREAT BANDS
ONLY $5.00
ALL AGES
WELCOME

SCREAM 9353 — AUG 3
UNITED MUTATIONS

9:00 PM $5

WILSON CENTER — 15 & IRVING NW

Benefit and March for Amnesty International

with: Scream

King Face

Swiz

3

free this man he is you

please bring candles....

Saturday, July 25th
Matinee show $5
Johns Hopkins SAIS
1740 Mass. Ave. NW
(near DuPont Circle)

The Day's Activities
1PM - Teach-in/film showing w/ award-winning film "Your Neighbor's Son: The Making Of a Torturer"
2PM - Benefit concert w/ speakers, literature, videos (and, maybe, food)
4PM - Benefit concert march past appropriate embassies to draw attention to human rights abuses worldwide, to end by 10PM with short ceremony in Sheridan Circle - hope to see you there!

more info. 276-9768

"Better to light one candle than to curse the darkness"

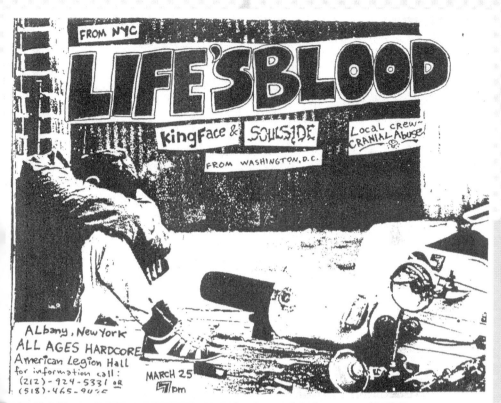

FROM NYC

LIFE'SBLOOD

KingFace & SOULSIDE   Local crew~
CRANIAL Abuse!

FROM WASHINGTON, D.C.

ALbany, New York
ALL AGES HARDCORE
American Legion Hall
for information call:
(212)-924-5331 or
(518)-465-94?6

MARCH 25
7pm

Kingface by Jason Buell

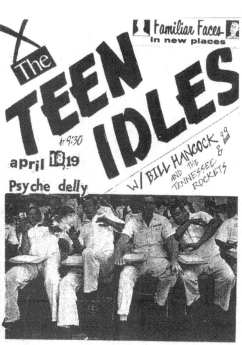

The TEEN IDLES

Familiar Faces in new places

at 9:30
april 18 19
Psyche delly

w/ BILL HANCOCK and the TENNESSEE ROCKETS 99

TEEN IDLES

w/ TRENCHMOUTH
JAN. 21 D.C. SPACE 7¢ N.W.

w/ BAD BRAINS
JAN. 26 MADAMS ORGAN

FROM D.C. VOID ⌶† PLUS SPECIAL GUESTS

AUG. 7 SAT.

GALLERY EAST 24 East St.
Near So. Station-   ALL
-Behind Hotel Essex   AGES

WITH: F.U.'S D.Y.S.

A BOMB SHOW

aND
⟨ HapPY NEw YeAR ⟩
WITH
ONE LAST WISH
AND
DAG NASTY

niteclub 9:30   8-21-86 $4!

RITES OF SPRING

FORT RENO PARK
LUNCHMEAT LAST SHOW   FREE
AUGUST 19 MONDAY 7:30 PM

HAPPY
HaPPydOLICKY
HappyGolicky

HAPPY GOLICKY

with
fire party
broken siren
              at foodforthought
6/21 early

MINOR THREAT
DOUBLE-O
BAD BRAINS
One of the last few...
SATURDAY, MAY 15
Irving Plaza 15th Street & Irving Place, NYC

OUT OF STEP

WASHINGTON DC PUNK INTERVIEWS
BY DAVID A. ENSMINGER

DESIGN BY WELLY ARTCORE AT CREATOR GRAPHICS

Made in the USA
Las Vegas, NV
08 September 2023